MOUNTAINS INTO GOLDMINES

Robert Schuller and the Gospel of Success

DENNIS VOSKUIL

GRAND RAPIDS, MICHIGAN
WILLIAM B. EERDMANS PUBLISHING COMPANY

Copyright © 1983 by William B. Eerdmans Publishing Company
255 Jefferson Ave. S.E., Grand Rapids, MI 49503

Library of Congress Cataloging in Publication Data

Voskuil, Dennis, 1944-
  Mountains into goldmines.

  1. Schuller, Robert Harold. 2. Reformed Church—
United States—Clergy—Biography. I. Title.
BX9543.S36V67 1983   285.7′32′0924 [B]   83-1729
ISBN 0-8028-3573-0

Dedicated to
my wife
Betty Trahms Voskuil
and my parents
Marion E. and Wallace C. Voskuil

CONTENTS

As the saga is told, it was 1955 when the Schuller bandwagon pulled out of Chicago and began rolling toward California. This westward trek was a singularly unimpressive sight: an old Chevrolet chugging along, carrying a young minister and his family toward the unknown. Like many who joined the great migration west following the Second World War, he brought little with him but a deep belief in himself and a fierce determination to make the best of new challenges and opportunities. But this was no ordinary young man on an ordinary quest for fame and fortune. This was a man who dreamed of a partnership with the Lord, in reaching the unchurched among the burgeoning population of southern California. He had an overwhelming yearning to establish a great church and build a mighty ministry.

Robert Harold Schuller has seen his dream come true. His ministry in California has prospered, even perhaps beyond his own expansive expectations. The church which he organized in a drive-in theater has mushroomed into a remarkable, vital, and innovative church of 10,000 members. Established in the open air, the congregation is now housed in the Crystal Cathedral, one of the truly spectacular ecclesiastical edifices of our time.

Schuller's influence, however, has spread far beyond Southern California. In part, this influence can be attributed to the popular church growth institutes which Schuller established as a means of spreading the secrets of his own success. But, above all, Schuller has become known as the smiling, animated preacher on one of America's most popular weekly religious telecasts. It has been through "Hour of Power" that Schuller has extended his influence across North America and the remainder of the English-speaking world. Considering the various facets of his successful ministry it is little wonder that *The Christian Century* recently ranked Schuller among the most prominent religious figures in America.*

This book deals with the Schuller phenomenon, the amazing ecclesiastical success story which began so inauspiciously in Southern California three decades ago. It is not a biography, however, for it is not my purpose to study the person of Robert Schuller, but to come to grips with his ministry and the positive message which gives form and focus to that ministry. Schuller's ecclesiastical success story, in a very real sense, is a paradigm of the very gospel of success which he proclaims through books, the growth institutes, and "Hour of Power."

As an exponent of "possibility thinking," Schuller's ideological lineage can be traced back through a long line of popular religionists in America who have stressed health and happiness through mind-conditioning. Closely linked to possibility thinking is Schuller's theology of self-esteem, which he has boldly introduced as the ideological basis for a "new reformation," which will center upon human needs.

With a message that emphasizes optimism, individual autonomy, positive thinking, and success, Schuller epitomizes much of that which has come to be defined as unique to American religion. As one who so truly reflects the American ethos, we should not be surprised at the popularity of his ministry. As an historian of American religion, I find that Schuller is especially significant and intriguing when he is placed within the broad context of American religion.

It is not my sole intent to describe and analyze the

* "Naming the Influentials," *The Christian Century* 99 (Jan. 6-13, 1982): 3-4.

ministry of Robert Schuller—the Garden Grove experiment, the growth institutes, the Crystal Cathedral, and "Hour of Power"—and the messages which undergird that ministry —possibility thinking and the theology of self-esteem. Rather, I will also describe Schuller's relationship to the perenially popular positive thinkers in American religious thought. And because the initial impetus for writing this book came from so many Christian friends who were truly wondering about the theological implications of Schuller's message, a final chapter has been written which serves as an assessment of Schuller's thought.

This book could not have been written without the generous assistance of various colleagues, friends, and family members. It has been my privilege to work in a stimulating and supportive intellectual environment at Hope College. Charles A. Huttar, David G. Myers, and Carol Bechtel Reynolds dissected the entire manuscript at a crucial stage— kindly but frankly suggesting important revisions. I am deeply indebted to them for their tough love. My colleagues in the Religion department—Elton J. Bruins, Wayne G. Boulton, Robert Palma, Richard and Christiana van Houten, Allen Verhey, and Henry Voogd—all helped me to clarify my thinking in various faculty seminars. I also want to thank Christopher Barney, Eugene P. Heideman, I. John Hesselink, Lynn Winkels Japinga, Mildred W. Schuppert, M. Eugene Osterhaven, Richard C. Oudersluys, and Gordon J. Van Wylen for reading through various chapters. I owe special thanks to Dr. Robert H. Schuller for two interviews, and to his staff for interviews which helped me to appreciate and understand the Schuller phenomenon; to Jon Pott and Sandra Nowlin, of Eerdmans Publishing Company, who edited the manuscript under difficult circumstances; to Marian Van Ry for faithfully deciphering my cryptic script and typing too many versions of the manuscript; to my father, Wallace C. Voskuil, a retired editor, who polished his craft again; to my wife, Betty Trahms Voskuil, editor, typist, proof-reader, who supported me through the entire project; and to my children, Derek, Karsten, and Elizabeth, who wondered if Daddy would ever finish writing his book.

March 25, 1983   Dennis N. Voskuil

MOUNTAINS INTO GOLDMINES

CHAPTER I

Scars into Stars:
The Making of a Possibility Thinker

America loves success stories. And no one has a better story to tell than Robert Schuller, the ecclesiastical giant who began his ministry preaching to fifty cars from the top of a tarpaper shack at a drive-in theater in Southern California. A promoter of the gospel of success through "possibility thinking," Schuller is his own best example. It is no wonder, then, that he so often retrieves vignettes from his past to underscore his message of self-help.

Recalled to teach and inspire, these autobiographical sketches have been carefully styled and shaped for the market of mass communication. This does not mean that Schuller has twisted history to satisfy pedagogical purposes. Rather, Schuller's recollections of his past so plainly cohere with his message that contradictions and inconsistencies are resolved and absorbed into the dominant theme. Schuller's own story and possibility thinking are fortuitously intertwined. Autobiography serves as pedagogy.

If the main theme of Schuller's ministry is "success through possibility thinking," the sub-theme is "turning scars into stars." Again Schuller draws upon his life's story, testifying that every obstacle has been turned into an opportunity, every pain into gain, and every trial into triumph. In many respects, his life sounds like an updated version of the once-popular "rags-to-riches" stories of Horatio Alger: poor farm boy from northwest Iowa becomes pastor of one of the greatest churches in America through prayer, persistence, and possibility thinking. Schuller is a true believer. And having tasted the fruits of the gospel of success, he is eager to share his good news. Like all effective

3

evangelists, Schuller communicates a message which has become an elaboration of his personal experiences.

Normally, the retelling of the Schuller saga begins in California, with the young pastor struggling to organize his drive-in church. When the whole story is told, however, it becomes apparent that the road to success was paved with many obstacles and opportunities long before it reached California. To understand Schuller, his message, and his ministry, we must follow that road back to its origin in the Midwest during the twenties.

Robert Harold Schuller was born at Alton, Iowa, on September 16, 1926, but reared on a farm near the hamlet of Newkirk, nine miles north of Alton (population 1,018), on the rich black soil of the northwest edge of the state. A typical four-corner Iowa farm community, Newkirk has changed very little since Schuller was a child—"a general store on one corner, a church on the next corner, the school on the third corner" and "a great big cornfield" on the fourth.[1]

Like most of their neighbors, the Schullers (or *Skullers*, as the folk in Iowa pronounce the name) belonged to that stock of hardy Dutch immigrants attracted to the area in the late 1800's by some of the most fertile cropland in America, and by the opportunity to establish a colony where they could practice their Calvinistic faith without interference from the state. These Iowans were part of a large wave of Dutch immigrants who settled in the Midwest—especially Western Michigan, Eastern Wisconsin, Northern Illinois, as well as Northwest Iowa—in search of religious freedom as well as economic betterment. In the Netherlands many had been members of De Gereformeerde Kerk, a schismatic communion which left the state church, De Hervormde Kerk, during the 1830's, convinced that it had become lax in upholding the Reformed principles set forth in various confessions of faith.

In America these immigrants first organized separate congregations but soon found a congenial home in the old Dutch Reformed Church, which proudly traced its heritage in this country to 1628, when Dominie Jonas Michaelius organized the first Dutch congregation in New Amsterdam. Today this congregation is part of the association of Reformed Churches in New York City that claims Marble Collegiate Church and Norman Vincent Peale. Convinced that the American branch of the Dutch Reformed had remained essentially pure in polity and doctrine, the new Dutch Americans yoked their congregations to that venerable denomination, renamed the Reformed Church in America. While the Eastern Reformed churches, located principally in New York and New Jersey, had by this time pretty well amalgamated into the mainstream of American Protestantism, the Midwestern immigrants took comfort in the fact that the old American denomination held steadfastly to the familiar confessions of the Dutch Reformation—the Heidelberg Catechism, the Belgic Confession, and the Canons of the Synod of Dort. In polity and practice, the Reformed Church is a Dutch cousin of the Presbyterian Churches in America. In general, however, the more recent nineteenth-century Dutch immigrants have held to a more orthodox interpretation of Calvinism. In the Midwest, at least, the Reformed Church is theologically epitomized by the acronym T.U.L.I.P.—total depravity, unlimited election, limited atonement, irresistible grace, and the perseverence of the saints. The emphasis is strongly upon divine sovereignty and grace over against human autonomy and efficacy. Typified by doctrinal purity rather than by evangelistic fervor, the R.C.A. has been strong and stable but has remained small, claiming 350,000 baptized members in 1980.[2]

Anthony and Jennie Schuller were faithful members of the Newkirk Reformed Church, and later the First Reformed Church in nearby Orange City, two of many congregations organized by the Dutch immigrants in Northwest

Iowa to serve as bulwarks of Reformed orthodoxy. Here they brought young Robert, the last of their five children, to be nurtured on the milk of the gospel as interpreted through the confessions of the church. Here he listened to sermons which stressed human depravity and divine judgments, repeated the Ten Commandments, and memorized questions and answers from the Heidelberg Catechism.

The religious nurture young Robert received at church was strongly reinforced at home. But while both parents shaped his perspective, Schuller probably owes his drive and determination more to his mother than to his father. A respected but not particularly prominent member of the farm community, Anthony Schuller is portrayed by granddaughter Sheila as a gentle, thoughtful, and compassionate man possessed of a simple and devout faith. Jennie, by contrast, is pictured as a woman of initiative, persistence, and vision, who sought to realize her own dreams through her youngest son:

> Grandma pushed Dad when he didn't feel like moving, and she inspired him to keep looking up. She taught him to do his very best and—most of all—never, *never* give up. It was from her drive that Dad learned to be industrious.[3]

It is not surprising that the Schullers dreamed of Robert's becoming a minister. There was no higher calling. In fact, Schuller's father dedicated his fifth child to the Lord even before he was conceived. On Sheila's account, the tired farmer knelt in a newly plowed furrow, lifted his face to the heavens, and prayed:

> O Lord, I know my Jennie is past her child-bearing years, but please plant one more seed—in my Jennie. And let it grow and bear a son—a son who will be a minister— who will in turn plant seeds, your seeds of love, in many hearts.[4]

Robert Schuller may not have known of his father's

prayer, but he certainly knew what his family and his pastor were hoping. And if that weren't enough, he could later recall the visit of his uncle Henry Beltman, a missionary who had served the church in China. As Schuller relates this pivotal experience, Uncle Henry, "tall, very handsome, and terribly alive with energy," bounded out of his car, ran up to him, ruffled his hair, and said, "Well! I guess you're Robert! I think you are going to be a preacher someday." That night the impressionable five-year-old secretly prayed, "Dear God, make me a preacher when I grow up!"[5] "I believe," Schuller has said, "that God made me a POSSI-BILITY THINKER then and there."[6] The would-be minister perfected his skills from the brow of a low hill overlooking the Floyd River, where he would be found "preaching enthusiastically" to a "congregation of cows and corn."[7]

But there were obstacles to overcome on the road to success. The Schuller family was poor. In a published sermon, "An Open Door to Prosperity," Schuller tells what it was like to grow up on an Iowa farm during the Great Depression:

> Until I was a senior in high school, we had no electricity, only kerosene lamps. Even after that we had no running water or storm windows. I remember waking the morning after a blizzard to find snow drifts in my bedroom because of cracks around the windows. We lived a very simple life, deriving our sustenance from the land. It was an earthy, pioneer kind of existence. Often there were no presents at Christmas time. And I grew up wearing my brother's hand-me-downs.[8]

Schuller is convinced that his very philosophy of life was shaped in part by his determination to overcome the trials of that era. He tells of dust storms that left people choking for air and black clouds that deposited "snowdrifts" of dirt along the country roads. Crops were devastated. One year during the thirties the drought was so severe that his father was able to harvest only half a wagon of ear corn from their 160-acre farm. Through it all, the family remained hopeful and refused to quit.[9]

The lessons in positive thinking which Schuller learned from his family during the years of drought were underscored during the mid-forties, when the farmstead was devastated by a tornado. Schuller, who was just home from college for the summer, remembers jumping into the family car with his parents to avoid the path of the twister and discovering later that all nine of the farm buildings had been sucked up by the whirling winds. But even then Anthony Schuller refused to throw in the towel. Dismantling an old house owned by a doctor in nearby Orange City and using the lumber to rebuild some of the sheds on the farm, he took the remaining insurance money and went to the bank to make payment on the mortgage—this to underscore the fact that he was not going to quit. Apparently impressed by his determination and courage, the bankers did not foreclose. It all paid off. During the next years the crops were bountiful and soon the mortgage was lifted. And young Robert had learned an important lesson in possibility thinking from his father:

> He taught me that it's almost impossible to be a loser unless you think and accept losing mentally. He had faith in the Lord and in nature itself. The sun is going to rise tomorrow, the sun is rising somewhere right now. This very minute there's a sunrise somewhere.[10]

Through all of this, the young man nurtured his dream of becoming a minister. School itself presented no small challenge, since he did not particularly enjoy his studies. As Sheila puts it: "Dad loved to preach, but the 'book-learning' was another story." Even in elementary school his mother "sternly prodded him to do his studying and reading."[11]

The reluctant student graduated from Newkirk High in 1943, at the age of sixteen, and promptly enrolled at Hope

College, 800 miles away in Holland, Michigan. A liberal arts school affiliated with the R.C.A., Hope was an ideal college at which to prepare for the ministry. There Schuller could pursue his life's dream. The decision to enroll at Hope he has never regretted. Here, he has said with pride, he first learned the meaning of excellence.[12] Hope has reciprocated by granting its famous graduate a Distinguished Alumnus Award in 1970 and an honorary doctorate in 1973.

Schuller was one of a very small number of male students at Hope College during the war years, having received a pre-seminary waiver from his draft board. A capable but undistinguished student, Schuller is remembered more for his musical talent, his organizational ability, and his self-confidence. As a very fine singer, Schuller helped to organize the Arcadian Four, a fraternity quartet which won all-college musical honors during his senior year. The Arcadian fraternity had been founded in 1946, when the glut of men returning from the armed forces swelled the ranks of the existing fraternities. The "Arkies" were composed almost entirely of pre-seminarians. These young men got a taste of the golden west in 1947, when Schuller convinced Hope President Irwin Lubbers to allow the quartet to make a gospel-singing tour with stops in Colorado, Iowa, Nebraska, and California. Sheila relates that it was while on this tour that her father fell in love with California. "This farm boy, who'd seen little more than cornfields, was awestruck by the palm trees, the orange trees, and the perennial sunshine. He decided right then and there that he'd be back."[13]

While it is doubtful that Schuller actually experienced the kind of grinding poverty so many other Americans knew during the Depression years, it is significant that he has genuinely perceived himself as living with the stigma of poverty. This was especially acute for him at Hope, where most of the students came from relatively well-off families.

While others could concentrate on academic, athletic, and social pursuits, Schuller had to take various college jobs to pay for tuition, room, and board. "I worked my way through college," he has said, "as a janitor cleaning toilets."[14]

Graduating from Hope College in 1947, Schuller entered Western Theological Seminary, just across the street. He might have chosen to attend the other denominational seminary in New Brunswick, New Jersey, but Western was the logical choice because it was closer to home and theologically more congenial to a conservative Midwesterner. Again Schuller did not particularly distinguish himself academically. He is remembered at Western as an average student but an excellent speaker who possessed a tremendous desire to succeed. Still, few who knew him then would have predicted that he would emerge as the eventual star of his class. For his Bachelor of Divinity thesis, Schuller prepared a 285-page scriptural and topical index for John Calvin's massive *Institutes of the Christian Religion*, a time-consuming task requiring comprehension as well as persistence. Indicating that he read through the *Institutes* ten times to finish the task, Schuller claims that this project has made him "an authority on John Calvin's theology."[15]

While in seminary, Schuller began to date Arvella De Haan, also from Newkirk but four years younger than he. They had neither dated nor really become acquainted before the young theolog came back to Iowa one weekend to preach at his home church. Arvella had become the church organist, and Schuller broke in on one of her practice sessions. Daughter Sheila writes that her father was instantly smitten by the woman peering at him from the organ bench. "Bill," he wrote to his best college friend after his first date, "I've met the girl I'm going to marry."[16]

It has been a happy partnership. A strong and talented woman, Arvella has been Schuller's best friend and most trusted advisor. In addition to having reared five children, she has been, from the beginning, program director of "Hour of Power." Her role in the Schuller success story has been large and impressive.[17]

During the eventful month of June 1950, Schuller married Arvella De Haan, graduated from Western Seminary, and was ordained as a minister in the Reformed Church in America. The ordination took place at the Ivanhoe Reformed Church in the Chicago suburb of Riverdale, Illinois. Ivanhoe was a fledgling congregation of around forty members which called the ambitious twenty-three year old to be their pastor with the hope that he could work a miracle of growth and renewal. This was just the sort of challenge for which Schuller had been waiting. During his senior year at seminary, he had written a paper on George Truett, a young pastor who had dedicated his life to making the struggling First Baptist Church of Dallas, Texas, into "the greatest church in America." When he retired forty years later, he left behind the largest Baptist church in the nation. Schuller now had a dream and Truett became his inspiration. He remembers asking God at the time:

> Give me a chance . . . to build a church from the bottom up. I covet no other man's job. I ask only for an opportunity to create a great job for myself, and leave behind something wonderful to bless generations yet unborn.[18]

Ivanhoe Reformed Church was certainly a congregation that would have to be built "from the bottom up." Composed of some persons who were staunchly Reformed in their orthodoxy and some who were new to the Reformed faith, Ivanhoe was being torn apart. Schuller remembers that the congregation was "split down the middle with suspicion and distrust," and that both factions tried to use him for their purposes. The young pastor was worn to a frazzle worrying about his church. On the verge of panic, Schuller "prayed desperately" for direction and strength.

11

Into his mind came the Bible verse: "All things work together for good to those who love God" (Romans 8:28), as well as the thought that God was trying to teach him something through the agonizing experience. Scars would be turned into stars. "Believe that God will let nothing happen to you unless something good will come out of your so-called trouble."[19]

Perhaps because it did not become the church of his dreams, Schuller says little about his work at Ivanhoe. It is apparent, however, that he was very effective in bringing the unchurched, at least those who were not members of a Reformed church, into the congregation. During his four-and-one-half-year ministry the church grew from forty to nearly four hundred members. One Sunday, those being received for membership outnumbered those who already claimed membership. It is certain, as Sheila writes, that Schuller had built a reputation around Chicago as a dynamic young minister.[20] He was convinced, however, that the situation at Ivanhoe was too restrictive and that the potential for growth was limited. Ivanhoe, he surmised, would not become "one of the greatest churches ever organized." So, when the Reformed Church's Classis of California beckoned him to organize a church in Garden Grove near Los Angeles, Schuller "leaped at the opportunity."[21] In California, a land bursting with opportunity, he would have a chance to build a truly great church. The Garden Grove Experiment was about to begin.

CHAPTER II

The Garden Grove Experiment

Southern California is America's last frontier, a mecca for the hardy individualists, the irrepressible dreamers, and the energetic entrepreneurs who felt strait-jacketed by traditional ways and conventional thinking back East where they had left their families. This was especially true after World War II, when favorable economic conditions encouraged a massive migration of opportunity seekers into the sunbelt culture of California. The situation fit Robert Schuller perfectly. In fact it is difficult to imagine the Schuller phenomenon as happening anywhere else.

"The Garden Grove Experiment"[1] is what Schuller himself likes to call his ministry in California. The label suits his pedagogical purposes, for it smacks not only of adventure but of adventure pursued with systematic, even scientific, rigor and consistency. So Schuller might be portrayed as a bold and courageous ecclesiastical scientist, with his laboratory the ethos of Southern California.

When the Classis of California decided to organize a new church in the Garden Grove area, it probably expected to build the church from a base of families with a Reformed background. A suburb of Los Angeles, Garden Grove was certain to grow rapidly in the following decade. All of the denominational demographers agreed that the area could easily support another Reformed Church. The Classis, therefore, searched for an ambitious young minister to do the job.

The Reverend Ray Beckering, who had known Schuller as a ministerial friend in the Chicago area and had left to take a pastorate in Los Angeles, suggested that the Classis contact his former colleague, who had done a fine job of building Ivanhoe in so short a time. Schuller immediately recognized his golden opportunity. He had remembered California from his touring days with the Arcadian Four. And so he took the train to Los Angeles to explore the possibilities.

Garden Grove immediately fired his imagination. He saw houses already springing up in the area but few churches to serve the burgeoning population. Asking God's guidance in the matter, he decided on the return trip to Chicago to accept the call:

> It was nearly midnight. Wide awake in the top bunk of the Santa Fe railroad car, I stared out the window. The train was stopped now, high in the Arizona mountains. A full moon fell on the snow-covered pines. Suddenly a deer leaped from behind a tree and bounded off into the moonlit night, spraying dry snow-dust in his trail. Then sparked by George Truett's experience, it came to me: the positive possibility thought, 'The greatest churches have yet to be organized.'[2]

When Schuller accepted the offer, he was given a salary of $4,000, a tiny parsonage in Garden Grove, and five hundred dollars seed money for the church. The Ivanhoe congregation had given the Schullers a farewell gift of four hundred dollars, which he invested in a small electric organ. Purchased from a friend in Sioux City, Iowa, while the family made their way to California—·four hundred dollars down and forty-five dollars a month for thirty-six months—it was to be delivered in California. Schuller was determined to begin his new ministry with an organ, something Ivanhoe did not have when he came to Chicago. Likewise, he was determined to use printed rather than mimeographed Sunday-morning bulletins.[3] Success—so goes one of the Schuller principles of church growth—feeds on the image of success.

As the saga is told, then, the Schullers arrived in California with these assets: five hundred dollars, an old Chevy, an electric organ, and a dream. (They arrived with two small children as well—Sheila, two years old, and Robert A., just six months. During the next few years, the family was to grow nearly as fast as the church, as the two older children made room for Jeanne, Carol, and Gretchen.) Against these meager assets, Schuller could list certain liabilities, not least of which was that he was working for a denomination which could claim only 350,000 baptized members nationwide, few of them in or around Garden Grove. When, like all good church-extenstion ministers, Schuller canvassed the area, he discovered that there were just two Reformed Church families. Even assuming a population explosion, he could expect no more than seventy-five Reformed families to move into the area during the next decade. How was he to succeed?

Well, it was clear that he would have to appeal to the unchurched. He would have to win over those people who had never before shown interest in organized religion. So, the denominational handicap turned out to be something of a boon, as Schuller was forced to abandon the conventional strategy of building a congregation upon denominational identity. He would have to reach the unchurched—and half of Orange County was unchurched. No doubt Schuller had already thought through this matter before he left Chicago, for just a week after arriving in California, he opened a bank account under the name "Garden Grove Community Church." Later he explained, "I didn't think the name 'Reformed' would bring the *unchurched* people rushing in!"[4] Schuller has continued to de-emphasize denominational identity throughout most of his ministry in California. While periodically pointing with pride to the fact that his church is connected to the venerable Reformed Church which traces its history back to 1628 in

New Amsterdam, he has put little accent upon denomina- tional ties. Until recently, his church has been Reformed only in small print. And in this respect he has been a model for a number of Reformed congregations which, in their ef- forts to disengage from an encumbering denominational identity—"Reformed from what?"—have become "Com- munity Churches." But in the past few years, Schuller has come to recognize the importance of being accountable to a stable mainstream denomination, and he has taken more interest in denominational affairs.

Schuller was faced with another more immediate prob- lem upon arriving in California. His still-to-be-gathered con- gregation had no place to worship. The traditional procedure for church extension was to rent a suitable building where Sunday services could be held until the congregation was established to the point where it could build permanent facilities. On his exploratory visit to California, the young pastor learned that few buildings were available in this booming Southern California real estate market. We are told that he practiced possibility thinking enroute to California by jotting down on a napkin a list of nine places which possibly could be rented for the services: (1) a school building; (2) an Elks Hall; (3) a mortuary chapel; (4) a Masonic Hall; (5) an empty warehouse; (6) a Seventh-Day Adventist Church; (7) a synagogue; (8) a drive-in theater; (9) an acre of ground for pitching a tent.

Within a week of his arrival, Schuller had exhausted the first seven possibilities on the list. It seems that the Presbyterians and Baptists had beaten him to the punch. So, he pursued the eighth option by asking the manager of the Orange Drive-in Theater if his place could be used for Sunday morning services. The manager obliged—at a cost of just ten dollars a Sunday, which would cover the cost of having a sound man throw the switch on and off.[5]

In another version of how the drive-in ministry began,

Sheila tells of the family's watching the movie *Cinderella* in the drive-in during the early days in California. Schuller was struck by the idea that the theater would be a perfect place for the worship services.[6] Although the story may vary slightly, the lesson remains the same: the power of prayer, persistence, and possibility thinking.

Having found a home for his church, Schuller began to spend the five hundred dollars seed money to prepare for the first worship service, scheduled for Sunday, March 25, exactly a month after his arrival. First, he constructed a four-by-eight-foot sign and set it under a palm tree in front of the drive-in, announcing that this would be the site of future church services. Next, he procured a microphone that would be jacked into the sound system of the theater. He also built an altar and a fifteen-foot cross to be placed on the tarpaper roof of the theater's snack bar, which would serve as a podium. A used trailer was purchased so that the electric organ could be transferred from the parsonage to the theater. Finally, aware of the need for advertisement, Schuller paid to have brochures printed which announced the new venture.

Included in the brochure was a glowing endorsement of the drive-in ministry from Norman Vincent Peale, the famous positive-thinking pulpiteer at the Marble Collegiate Church in New York City. Schuller had written for and received permission to quote extensively from a letter of support from Peale. While he had read some of Peale's sermons and was familiar with some of his best-selling books, Schuller was less interested at this point in identifying with Peale's message than with his popularity. Aware that Peale was the only minister in the Reformed Church who could attract the attention of the unchurched, Schuller "grabbed hold of his coattails."[7]

Despite Peale's endorsement, few of Schuller's ministerial colleagues were impressed with the drive-in idea.

17

One pastor, "the most sincere impossibility thinker" Schuller claims to have met, was incredulous that he would start a new church there. A theater was a "devil's den" and a "passion pit" and "couldn't possibly work." Schuller reminded his friend that Paul had preached on Mars Hill in Athens, hardly a holy spot. Other ministers expressed sympathy that Schuller would not have a building with pews and Sunday School rooms and that he would be located outside of downtown Garden Grove. Schuller countered by explaining that he had the advantages of accessibility (the drive-in was right off the busy Santa Ana Freeway), unlimited parking (room for 1,700 cars), and a larger market (the theater was at the intersection of three large cities—Anaheim, Garden Grove, and Santa Ana).

While there were moments when Schuller himself wondered whether the idea would work, he moved ahead, sensing that he was embarking upon a bold and exciting experiment. He bought space in the local newspapers and advertised immodestly:

> In three weeks we will be starting what will become Orange County's newest and most inspiring Protestant church. . . . Come as you are in the family car.[8]

Including members of a choir borrowed from a Los Angeles church, who were encouraged to drive in separate autos to help fill the cavernous drive-in, about fifty cars and a hundred people attended the inaugural service. Schuller preached through a microphone on top of that refreshment stand, his text taken from Matthew 17:20: "If you have faith as a grain of mustard you can say to this mountain, 'move,' and nothing will be impossible unto you." Arvella played the electric organ, which had been bolted to the deck of the used trailer. It was a typical Protestant service in atypical surroundings: the choir sang and an offering, totaling $83.75, was received at the appropriate time. When it was over, Schuller pronounced it a great success and the next morning typed up a glowing press release:

> Southern California's first Drive-In church got off the ground yesterday with an attendance of over half a hundred cars.[9]

Those who had predicted doom for the drive-in ministry proved to be wrong. Over the weeks, many hundreds of people were enticed by the chance to "Come as you are in the family car." The formula for success—an electric organ, printed bulletins, and plenty of publicity—was continued during the early years. And Schuller continued to clutch the coattails of Norman Vincent Peale. Some months after the first service, he wrote again to Dr. Peale, inviting him to preach at "the largest church in Orange County, with parking for 1,700 cars!" Peale's book *The Power of Positive Thinking* was still on the best-selling lists, and Schuller was convinced that the popular author-preacher would make a walloping impression on the people of Orange County.

Schuller's faith in Peale was amply rewarded. The pastor from New York drew more than 1,700 cars and 6,000 people. For more than twelve months after that service, hundreds of people attended the church who came originally to hear Dr. Peale "in person."[10] Schuller learned a lesson which he has employed with consistency: if you want an audience, invite popular guests.

The congregation was officially organized on September 27, 1958, six months after the inaugural service, and it grew rapidly. In traditional fashion, plans were made to build a church to house the burgeoning membership. Two acres were bought on Chapman Avenue west of the drive-in, and with the help of a loan secured from the extension fund of the Classis of California, a beautiful $70,000 structure was built. All assumed that once situated in the new building, the congregation (now about two hundred members) would abandon the drive-in. But there was the problem of what to do with Rosie Gray, a paralyzed member of the drive-in church who along with her husband had recently been baptized in their car. The congregation decided to hold two Sunday morning services, an early one at the chapel and a later one at the drive-in. It was assumed that Rosie would soon die and then the drive-in would be discontinued. But Rosie stubbornly did not die for four years. The problem of "what to do with Rosie" meant that there were basically two congregations which were growing separately and simultaneously. Thus, for four years, Schuller followed the same rigorous Sunday routine: a preaching service from 9:30–10:30 at the chapel on Chapman Avenue, and then, with Arvella and the kids packed into the old Chevy and the trailer with bolted-down organ careening behind, a mad dash to the drive-in for another service at 11:00.[11]

It is little wonder that, at this point, Schuller began to dream of merging the chapel with the drive-in ministry. Why not have people worship inside and outside at the same time? The idea was not entirely novel: discovering that his building was too small, a St. Petersburg, Florida, minister had put loudspeakers in the parking area. But in its scope and vision, Schuller's dream of a great drive-in walk-in church was bold and daring, the first of its kind in America. Schuller remembers how he envisioned the new facility:

> I could see a sanctuary with glass walls, gardens, fountains leaping in the sunlight, bells hanging in open towers, all rising from acres of tree-shaded grounds.

In a sermon entitled "How to Make Your Dreams Come True," Schuller used his idea of a drive-in walk-in church as an illustration, obviously hoping that the members in his congregation would be excited by the same vision of glass, gardens, bells, and towers. Many did come to share the dream, but others did not, and in the end the issue split the congregation.[12]

At a congregational meeting called soon after the "Dream" sermon, Schuller presented three possible solutions to the problem facing the church: (1) divide into two autonomous churches; (2) drop the drive-in ministry; (3) merge the two groups on a new piece of property into a drive-in walk-in church. After candid debate, Dr. Wilfred Landrus, a true possibility thinker according to Schuller, rose and read a motion he had written on a scrap of paper:

> Mr. Chairman, I move that this congregation under God go on record as favoring merger, and that we authorize the consistory to conduct further study toward acquiring property for this purpose.

Upon further discussion, the congregation passed Landrus's motion by a relatively slim margin, 55-46. With an eye for history, Schuller later retrieved the piece of paper upon which the motion had been scribbled.[13]

Soon afterward, following another "narrow and noisy vote," the congregation decided to buy ten acres of land for $6,600 an acre, $18,000 down and $400 a month for fifteen years. A furious fund-raising effort ensued to meet the 120-day deadline for the down payment. Schuller left no stone unturned in his effort to find funds, borrowing from his family in Iowa and even cashing in his life insurance policies. On the 120th day, with four hours to go before the escrow office would be closed, Schuller was still $3,000 short of the necessary $18,000 down payment.

Having exhausted all apparent possibilities, Schuller disconsolately called his wife admitting defeat. Arvella suggested that he contact Rosie Gray's husband, Warren, who had already contributed $2,000. Schuller was hesitant to do this since Gray had just returned from the hospital after discovering that he was filled with incurable cancer. But he made the call and Warren Gray agreed to come up with the remaining $3,000. Schuller met the "ashen-faced and hollow-eyed" Gray at his bank, received the money from the cashier, and rushed to the escrow company. *"Sixty minutes before the deadline,"* he writes excitedly, *"God took title to His ten acres of land."*[14] In a story which reads like the *Perils of Pauline*, Schuller's dream was saved at the brink of disaster by persistence, pluck, and Warren Gray.

God's "ten acres" were in hand, but the congregation continued to battle over the merger issue. Since the sale of the Chapman chapel property required approval from the Classis of California, a meeting was called to discuss such a sale. Here some members of his congregation spoke against the sale of the chapel and "Schuller's plan," as it had come to be called. After heated debate, during which, in Schuller's words, "a few tradition-bound churchmen" sided with the Garden Grove dissidents, the classis decided to authorize selling the chapel property. During the closing prayer, five prominent members of Schuller's church walked out of the meeting, and when he arrived at his office the next morning, he learned that the clerk of consistory, the church treasurer, the vice-president of the church, and his personal secretary had all resigned. This capped nearly two years of intense opposition to Schuller's plan, during which some members had met secretly to plan ways to torpedo the proposed merger.

Schuller admits that this was his valley of despair in the ministry. Sensitive to criticism, he suffered keenly under the opposition to his leadership. "I would have relished nothing more than a fatal heart attack," he says. "In that way, I would have been removed with honor from the unhappy scene!"[15]

Unable to shake his despair, Schuller found in prayer a significant discovery—it was time to turn over the headship of Garden Grove Church to Jesus Christ:

> I may have been over-dramatic but the truth is I stepped out of my chair, stretched out an open hand to my empty seat and said, 'Then Lord, You sit there. If You want this walk-in drive-in church to be built, that's wonderful. And if for some reason You don't want this dream to materialize, I'll accept that too. Right now I'll be immensely relieved if You will please take command.'

Schuller remembers that he turned, walked out of his office, and left for a scheduled vacation confident that the dream was now in the Lord's hands. When he returned from vacation, the mountain began to move. A dissident assistant pastor had accepted a call to another church, the chapel was sold at a profit, and the architectural plans for the new church were approved.[16]

The architect secured to design the million-dollar structure was Richard Neutra, a highly respected advocate of "bio-realism" who came to have a profound impact upon Schuller and his ministry. Neutra believed that buildings should assist in bringing people close to nature, which he understood to be a marvelous tranquilizing system. As Neutra told Schuller:

> When I design your church it will be planned so close to nature that we will give to the Creator a chance to use the built-in tranquilizing system again. We shall block out the ugly power line with solid walls; we shall throw open windows to the big sky! We shall bring the gentle sound of water into the place of peace. Tranquilized, relaxed, we shall be receptive to the natural flow of God's creative thoughts.[17]

Neutra's architectural style, with its use of glass walls, lush vegetation, water fountains, reflecting pools, and vertical stone masonry,[18] beautifully complemented a ministry which stresses peace of mind through possibility thinking.

It took two years to raise the funds and finish the monumental project, but by the fall of 1961, the drive-in walk-in church was completed. "The great glass cathedral" seated a thousand people (later the building was expanded to accommodate 1,700), and the drive-in parking lot equipped with hi-fi speakers held 500 cars. When it was finished, Schuller again turned to Norman Vincent Peale to preach the first sermon. It was a moment to be relished and remembered:

> [Dr. Peale] mounted the pulpit and looked across a drive-in parking area filled with five hundred cars carrying nearly two thousand worshippers. He looked across the upholstered pews of the sanctuary crowded with over one thousand people. The choir sang "Holy, Holy, Holy." I pressed a button—and two twenty-five-foot-high sections of glass wall alongside the pulpit separated slowly like angel's wings opening. Now the minister in the pulpit could look clearly out at both the walk-in and drive-in worshippers. It worked. Beautifully. Over four thousand people that were there were sure—this was a success. A handful of POSSIBILITY THINKERS had tested and proved the reality of POSSIBILITY THINKING.[19]

With the completion of this masterfully functional structure, the Garden Grove Community Church would begin to grow at a stunning rate. By the end of the sixties it could boast a membership of 5,000. A decade later the figure had doubled. The unique concept of a drive-in walk-in church also brought national publicity to the church. *Newsweek, Time,* and other national publications began to notice Schuller and his congregation.[20] Much of the coverage was superficial and cynical, but Schuller clearly had found a formula for success which he was not about to alter in the face of criticism.

In 1965, Schuller preached another version of the sermon "How to Make Your Dreams Come True." He was about to pursue another grand project. He announced his vision of building a tower fourteen or fifteen stories high that would house the growing church staff, a psychological counseling clinic, a twenty-four-hour-a-day telephone counseling center, and a chapel. The "little chapel in the sky," he promised, would be a "twinkling diamond of hope in the black, night sky at the freeway hub of this great county." It would become a "tower of hope" that would say to the public that "there is an eye that never closes, there is an ear that never shuts, there is a heart that never grows cold."[21]

Again there was internal opposition to Schuller's dream. The idea survived, however, and after initial fund drives the congregation decided to borrow the money needed to finish the project. The Tower of Hope was officially dedicated in September of 1968 by Norman Vincent Peale, who had also participated in the ground-breaking ceremonies two years earlier. Peale's presence was especially appropriate. He had established his own psychiatric clinic in New York City more than thirty years before. Convinced that mental therapy and the gospel are closely linked, both Schuller and Peale have placed psychology at the center of their ministries.

At 8:00 p.m. on the day of its dedication, the twenty-four-hour telephone counseling service went into operation. By dialing N-E-W H-O-P-E, any person around the country could receive counsel from a trained volunteer staff of two hundred. During the first year more than 10,000 calls were received, and by 1980 the annual figure had risen to more than 50,000.[22] Topped by a ninety-foot cross which is lighted at night, the Tower of Hope is the tallest building in Orange County. "The eye that never closes" overlooks Disneyland, Knotts Berry Farm, and Angels Stadium.

Schuller's penchant for dreaming expansive and expensive dreams did not end with the completion of the Tower of Hope. Already during the early seventies, it had become apparent that the church would restrict growth unless it was able to seat more than the 1,700 people who regularly attended the two major Sunday morning services, which were being taped for national viewing as the "Hour of Power'' television program. Convinced that ''the shoe must not tell the foot how large to grow,'' Schuller guided the congregation through two major studies of the problem. Among the proposed solutions: a major expansion of the existing sanctuary, which would cost two million dollars, and constructing a rather ordinary new church which would cost five million dollars.[22a] Unenthused by such proposals, Schuller dusted off his ''dream'' sermon and challenged the congregation with his vision of a massive glass cathedral which would seat 4,000 people and serve as a monument of faith for centuries to come. The scope and cost of the project (originally estimated at seven million dollars) must have staggered some of the leaders of the Garden Grove Church, but they had grown accustomed to such visions from their pastor. The congregation agreed to pursue the dream.

Chosen to design Schuller's vision was Phillip Johnson, one of the most prominent architects in America. Early in his career, Johnson belonged to the school of reductionistic modernism epitomized by Mies van der Rohe, his great mentor. But something of a maverick in his profession, Johnson later broke with van der Rohe and in his iconoclastic brilliance ''held out for architecture as an art in a period when many other architects were trying to make it an instrument of social salvation.''[23] He had designed a number of highly acclaimed structures: the Glass House in New Canaan, Connecticut; the A. T. & T. building, New York; the Dade County (Florida) Cultural Center; Pennzoil Place, Houston; the IDS Center, Minneapolis; and the Fort Worth Water Garden.

It was the Fort Worth Water Garden, a five-block landscape project, which brought Johnson to Schuller's attention. During a flight to Finland in August of 1975, Arvella ran across a picture of the project in *Vogue* magazine. Impressed, she alerted her husband who had never heard of

26

Johnson and assumed that he was a landscape artist. A week later, however, he read an article which listed Johnson as one of the world's great architects. Encountering the architect's name twice in one week seemed a divinely-inspired coincidence, and so the next time he was in New York, Schuller called Johnson's firm. Johnson was out of town and John Burgee, his partner, was out for lunch, but Schuller left a message and then showed up in the afternoon unannounced. When Burgee returned from lunch he told his secretary that he wanted to dodge Schuller. The Californian, he assumed, was looking for a job. When the misunderstanding was cleared up and Burgee understood that Schuller was looking for someone to design a multimillion-dollar church, the pastor received a gracious reception. Burgee showed Schuller photographs of the firm's work, but Schuller hardly looked at them. "I have only one question," he said upon leaving. "Do you think I will have a spiritual experience with Mr. Johnson?"

When they finally met, Schuller discovered that although Johnson claimed not to be a religious person, the two were on a harmonious wave length, one that was "transcendent enough to be labelled a spiritual relationship."[24] So Schuller commissioned Johnson and his partner to design "the ultimate worship center" for Garden Grove. In less than three months, Johnson and Burgee proposed a solid-wall building with a pitched glass roof. Schuller was disappointed. He told the architects that they should rid themselves of preconceptions about what is good and proper religious architecture. Then, recalling his lessons in "bio-realism" from Richard Neutra, Schuller suggested a building entirely of glass. Having begun his ministry in the open air of a drive-in theater, Schuller told the architects, he did not want a building in which he felt visually entrapped. "I wanted a sense of freedom for the human spirit. Man was designed to worship in nature." As Schuller put it later, "Theoretically we don't want to have a building at all."[25]

Johnson returned to California a few months later with a design for a spectacular all-glass building. Shaped like a four-pointed star which stretches to 415 feet long and 207 feet wide, the building would soar 128 feet high. Inside, the space would be open and expansive as the structure would be framed and supported by an intricate series of web-like trusses. Absolutely free of "walls," the skeleton would be wrapped by more than 10,000 window panes, allowing the congregation to commune with nature while being protected from its vicissitudes. With main floor and balconies, the church would seat just 3,000 persons, but many hundreds more would be able to see and hear the services from their cars through huge glass doors that would open to the left of the pulpit.

Schuller was ecstatic. From that time until construction was completed, the design of the building remained essentially unchanged. Even when faced with great pressure to reduce the size of the structure to save on construction costs, Schuller remained steadfast. It would be a desecration of the new building, he was convinced, to lose the long clean sweep of that design. "I'm willing to give up space for myself on the podium, but I will not compromise on a single detail of this plan."[26]

Having settled on the design, Schuller now faced the task of raising funds to pay for construction. He had hoped that the building would cost about seven million dollars to complete, but skyrocketing inflation rates quickly drove up the projected construction costs. By mid-1977, the estimated costs had reached ten million dollars. This was disheartening news, but Schuller prayed and reached back for some possibility-thinking miracles. Despite the rising costs the project would not be abandoned. Already a bank loan of three and one-half million dollars had been secured and some major gifts had been promised, including a million dollars from W. Clement Stone and another million from a supporter in California. Then in August of that year, the contractor informed Schuller that the price would come to nearly fifteen million dollars. At this point, Schuller was devastated. He tells us that he even prepared a news release announcing that the project would have to be abandoned. But in this moment of defeat, Schuller received encouragement from his friends and from a Catholic nun who, inspired by the plans for the Crystal Cathedral, became determined to build the wing of a hospital.[27]

Buoyed, Schuller hung on to his dream, and groundbreaking ceremonies took place December 4, 1977. The occasion called for a new version of "How to Make Your Dreams Come True." The ceremony boosted Schuller's morale, but it didn't cure his financial woes as the soaring inflation rate drove the building costs to nearly twenty million dollars before the structure was completed in 1980.

During construction, every effort was made to guarantee enough funds to keep the project on target. Occasionally, major donations were made—notably an unsolicited gift of one million dollars from an anonymous donor in Chicago, who later contributed another million dollars; both gifts came during critical stages in the construction process. Schuller believes that such gifts were provided by God. Later, when the building was nearly finished, Hazel Wright gave a million dollars to build a massive organ which would combine pipes from two existing organs (a Fratelli-Rufatti built in Italy and the Aeolian-Skinner removed from Lincoln Center in New York). A number of major donations came in, but the project was also sustained throughout by those many "little people" who had come to share Schuller's vision of faith and hope. In the end, more than 10,000 persons contributed to the building fund. Many of them were viewers of "Hour of Power" who purchased window panes, steel girders, and mylar stars which were eventually hung from the top of the structure. Members of the Garden Grove Church backed construction with constant contributions. Schuller demonstrated his unwavering commitment to the project during a crucial period by selling his own inheritance and challenging the leaders of his congregation to make similar sacrifices.[28]

Finally, in an effort to pay off the construction debt before the September 1980 dedication, Schuller came up with the ingenious scheme of asking Beverly Sills, the popular opera singer, to give one of her last recitals before retirement at the nearly finished cathedral. The seats for this performance would cost $1,500 apiece. Schuller sent letters of invitation to the 10,000 members of the church, the 800,000 families on his "Hour of Power" mailing list, as well as to some of his close friends and admirers, such as Frank Sinatra and Glenn Ford. The response was overwhelming: all of the 2,862 seats were sold out well before the concert.[29]

The concert was a financial success for Schuller—over four million dollars were raised—but an acoustical disaster for the Crystal Cathedral. Miss Sills, who received $15,000 for her performance, gave the audience two hours of Vivaldi, Schubert, and Rossini, but her words were distorted and blurred, in great part because she was performing in an unfinished building and through a makeshift sound system. The next day the music critics unfairly informed the world that the Crystal Cathedral was "the world's fanciest 10,000 window echo chamber." The Sills performance, declared one critic, "bore no resemblance to art. . . . She might just as well have been singing in a windswept cave, or under water, or on a short wave radio from Timbuktu." Another wrote that the recital was "a sonic Kafka nightmare, a surreal bath of echoes." Miss Sills understood the reasons for the echo-distorted performance, and even joked about it fifteen days later when she told Johnny Carson and millions watching "The Tonight Show" that her voice could still be heard in the Crystal Cathedral.[30]

The national joke that "people who build glass churches shouldn't give concerts" didn't really bother Schuller. The concert did pay off the remaining construction costs. And besides, great cathedrals are supposed to echo, aren't they? Another criticism did bother Schuller, however—the charge of poor stewardship. As the Crystal Cathedral project moved toward completion, it attracted ever increasing national publicity. *Time, Newsweek,* and newspapers from across the country sent reporters to see the structure and talk to the man who inspired its construction. Schuller's dream sparked the interest of the TV networks, and he was featured on "60 Minutes" and the nightly news programs; he was also interviewed by Phil Donahue and Mike Douglas. And with this surge of national publicity came a massive wave of criticism.

The criticism centered on the fact that a Christian church was spending twenty million dollars to construct an opulent building in a needy world. How could such a project be justified in 1980? Across the country, letters to the editor expressed dismay and disgust. Especially in the religious press, writers questioned Schuller's motives, wondering whether this building was a monument to Schuller or to God. An article in the *Church Herald,* the denominational magazine of Schuller's own Reformed Church, stated that the Crystal Cathedral represented a distortion of the Christian understanding of success. Wendell Karsen, a Reformed Church missionary, then related a melodramatic modern parable which told of poor people around the world being enraged by and ultimately destroying a glass cathedral of materialism and self-indulgence.[31]

Schuller had expected some criticism and recounts a private conversation he had with God when the project was facing financial problems. "God, if you want it built, provide the cash and I'll take the criticism." He admitted that the structure appeared to be expensive—but only from a short-sighted perspective. Like the great cathedrals in Europe, this one would last for hundreds of years, and therefore end up being one of the cheapest church buildings of our times. "You simply divide the number of days of its lifespan into the dollar figure and it only adds up to a few pennies a day! The structures which last only 20 to 60 years are really the most expensive!" In another method of cost-accounting, Schuller points out that the structure weighs twenty-four million pounds, which divided by the twenty-million-dollar price tag, comes to less than a dollar a pound—less than hamburger![32]

Defending the building from another angle, Schuller claims that it is cost efficient, "a money-generating factory" which will produce millions for missions over the next few decades. Like any viable business, the church must spend money to make money. Certain that the Crystal Cathedral will attract more members and more viewers who will contribute more money to the mission of the church, he is convinced that the venture is fiscally responsible. Schuller does not deny that the Crystal Cathedral is an expensive monument, but he insists that because the structure attracts people and inspires them to build beautiful lives, it is a *functional* monument. "There's a place for monuments," he says. "And if the monument can be an instrument, you've got a winner."[33]

Responding to critics who have charged that the Crystal Cathedral is extravagant, Schuller has argued that pedestrian architecture can be responsible for pedestrian faith. "Doctrinaire architecture is probably a major cause for Protestantism's decline." Considering himself a patron of the arts, Schuller believes that he has helped to build a lasting monument to God which rivals Notre Dame and the other medieval cathedrals. A church building, he reasons, should be an expression of faith which is glorious and expansive. Architect Johnson thinks that he has designed a building which meets Schuller's grand religious vision. "I think architecture should really be done *ad majorem dei gloriam*, to the greater glory of God." Obviously pleased with the space which he created under glass, Johnson wants the Crystal Cathedral to be understood as the crowning achievement of his career. He underscored this point when he quoted architect Erich Mendelsohn: "Architects are remembered for their one-room buildings," adding, "I hope to be remembered by this one."[34]

Schuller certainly has not satisfied all of his critics. Battles over congregational priorities and mission strategies have been waged since the day of Pentecost. Some argue against the construction of church buildings altogether, others believe that they may be built but must be as spare and functional as possible, and still others are convinced that people need majestic, inspiring edifices as expressions of faith. Like many age-old debates in the church, this one will continue long after the Crystal Cathedral has ceased to be a lively issue.[35]

Schuller blunted some of the criticism when he promised that the Cathedral would be dedicated debt-free, and that not a single undesignated dollar would come from the offering plate for the construction or maintenance of the building. Once dedicated, every offering taken in the Crystal Cathedral would be used "to minister to hurting people around the world." Indeed the first offering received in the new building (more than one hundred thousand dollars) was designated for the construction of a hospital in Chiapas, Mexico, near the Guatamalean border. This medical center was advertised as the first in a series of "Good Samaritan Inns" which are to be established around the world.[36] Whether this new dream will catch the imagination of those who contributed to the construction of the Crystal Cathedral is an open question. Schuller may discover, as have other church leaders, that people give more readily to masonry than to missions.

The Crystal Cathedral was officially unveiled on September 14, 1980. During this day, which Schuller called the happiest in his life ("It transcends my highest expectations"), thousands attended the services at Garden Grove and millions more watched on television. The national news media were on hand for the occasion, and generally they were impressed. Some observers praised it as "the religious building of the century." *Newsweek* reported that it was "one of the most spectacular religious edifices in the world." The thousands of visitors who were already making the Crystal Cathedral one of the most popular tourist sites in Southern California seemed to agree that the building was one of the visual wonders in America. When he first viewed the impressive structure, the witty Norman Cousins reportedly remarked: "That's the kind of church God would build—if he could afford it."[37]

Architectural critics were impressed as well. Johnson's building was applauded more than anything else for its expansive and explosive space. While the critics noted that the building lacked that aura of mystery that epitomized the great cathedrals of the Middle Ages, it was viewed as a perfect expression of modern religion. Open, expressive, uplifting, the building provided a fitting stage for Schuller's ministry. Said Paul Goldberger, critic for the *New York Times*:

> If this is not the deepest or the most profound religious building of our time, it is at least among the most entertaining—one that will do much to interest a public that has grown accustomed to thinking of churches as banal works of architecture and not as uplifting ones. Here at Garden Grove, the goals of religion and the goals of architecture are united, as earnestly as they were in ages past; the result tells more than a little about the priorities of each of these pursuits in our time.[38]

34

In 1980, the Garden Grove Community Church changed its official name to the Crystal Cathedral of the Reformed Church in America.

CHAPTER III

Sharing the Secrets of Success

Success breeds imitation. The success of the Garden Grove Experiment inevitably has propelled Schuller into the forefront of the church growth movement. Eager to emulate his ministry, many have asked him to reveal his formula for building such a great church. A faithful missionary of the gospel of growth, Schuller has eagerly obliged, supplying exhaustive blueprints for success. In this chapter we will examine Schuller's plans for building church membership— his foundational philosophy as well as his practical techniques for growth.

The church growth movement in North America is normally traced to the publication of Donald McGavran's *Bridges of God* in 1955, the same year Schuller began his ministry in Garden Grove. McGavran's book triggered interest in the research and analysis of church growth principles. Initially, these studies focused upon growth in Third World countries, but during the early 1970's these principles caught the interest of church leaders in the United States and Canada. Spearheaded by a post-McGavran generation of growth experts, including Winifred Arn, Lyle Schaller, and C. Peter Wagner, and centered at Fuller Theological Seminary in California, the growth movement has become a vital force today in North America. And Schuller is generally credited as playing a significant role in the history of the movement. He not only provided a model for growth, he also implored American Christians "to think church growth."[1]

Garden Grove is one of the ecclesiastical success stories of our time. So Schuller, a religious entrepreneur, and not one to hide his light under a basket, has gone into the business of sharing the secrets of his success. In 1969, he organized the Robert H. Schuller Institute for Successful Church Leadership. Headed by Wilbert Eichenberger, the four-day Institutes are generally held three times a year with an average enrollment of two hundred, mostly pastors, their wives, and church lay leaders. The participants pay about two hundred dollars plus meals and lodging for the opportunity of attending diagnostic clinics and how-to workshops, but the central features are five finely-tuned, humorous, and theologically oriented presentations in which Schuller expounds the principles of church growth which he tested at Garden Grove.

Schuller's message of church growth has been successfully popularized by his Institutes. Over the years more than 15,000 people have come to conferences at Garden Grove. Those attending the Institutes come from a wide range of religious traditions in America, from free-church evangelicals to high-church Episcopalians. The workshops have been endorsed by a number of the giants of the American church, including Billy Graham. From the beginning, the growth experts have lauded the Institutes. McGavran himself has commended them for "helping to turn static middle class American denominations around" and Wagner lauds it as "a truly pace setting support source for pastors . . . unsurpassed as a church growth training program available today."[2]

During the last few years, a version of the Institute has gone on the road. The five Schuller lectures have been filmed and shown to church groups around the country. Each participant at the film workshop pays about twenty-five dollars to see the films and participate in various seminars and workshops which focus upon growth in particular congregations. Schuller's secrets have been made even more widely accessible in a book entitled *Your Church*

Has Real Possibilities, which is an amplified version of the five Institute presentations. Convinced that he is marketing a workable formula for success, Schuller nearly offers a money-back guarantee in the Preface to the book:

> I know that some leaders who read these pages are to-day in a despairing time of life. I say to you, "Think with me—from chapter to chapter—and I believe God is go-ing to give you marvelous success, too! I absolutely guar-antee that if you will follow the prescriptions laid down in this book, your church will grow."[3]

The Institutes are best known for how-to formulas and practical principles, but Schuller's design for church growth is actually undergirded by two important philosophical as-sumptions. First, he assumes that growth is not only good but necessary. "It is a law of life that 'where there is no growing, there is dying.' Where there is growing, there is dynamic living. The church must either grow or perish."[4] Second, Schuller assumes that God wants his church to grow, but that growth must be prayed for, planned for, and worked for. It doesn't just happen. Like Charles Grandison Finney, the father of urban evangelism who believed that revivals were the "result of the right use of constituted means," Schuller holds that church growth is an applied science. The proper application of certain tested principles will bring expected results.

Something needs to be said here about Schuller's understanding of the role and function of the church. While he calls himself a Calvinist, he believes that the reformer was somewhat reactionary when it came to understanding the church. A Calvinistic definition of the church as "a place where the word is proclaimed, sacraments administered, and discipline maintained" is inadequate. Schuller defines the church as "a group of joyful Christians happily shar-ing their glorious faith with the despairing souls of their fellowmen who have never known the joy of Christ."[5] Viewing the local church as a "mission station," Schuller insists that it must put the needs and concerns of its members just one notch below the needs and concerns of those outside the membership. Church growth (outreach or evangelism) is not simply one of many church functions. It is the central function, the very pulse of the church.

These assumptions provide a foundation upon which Schuller builds a conceptual framework for church growth. According to Wilfred Bockelman, who has attended the Institutes at Garden Grove, there are five crucial emphases to the program. First, Schuller underscores the message of possibility thinking. We shall try to analyze this concept fully in a later chapter, but it is important to point out here that Schuller urges church leaders to break out of their growth-restricting negativism and dream larger dreams of success than they ever thought possible. Possibility thinking is a fresh perspective of faith that God will enable us to move mountains for his sake. With possibility thinking, one does not ask, "How much does it cost?" or "Can we afford it?" New programs must meet three simple and positive tests: (1) Would this be a good thing for God? (2) Would it help people who are hurting? (3) Is someone else doing the job? If the answer to the first two questions is "yes" and the answer to the last is "no," then the resources will be found to complete the project.[6] Readers and listeners are reminded that with possibility thinking, Schuller has built a 10,000-member congregation, two glass cathedrals, and a successful television ministry.

A second emphasis in Schuller's approach is the critical importance of strong pastoral leadership. He believes that the decline of the American church is directly related to the fact that pastors without power have been wallowing in despair and negativity.[7] Certain that organizations function best when power is delegated to those who can use it most effectively, he regrets that most churches are organized in such a way that leadership is left in the hands of the lay people—the part-timers. He insists that with rare exception even the most dedicated lay people consider the church to be the third priority in their life, after profession and family. On the other hand, the full-time local pastor places the church first.

Believing that "leadership is a full time business,"[8] Schuller counsels pastors to be strong leaders of their congregations. Following the constitutional requirements of the Reformed Church in America, Schuller serves as the president of the Consistory (composed of elected elders and deacons), which is mandated to make the final congregational decisions. He also serves as an ex-officio member of all committees with the power to appoint the chairpersons over those committees. While he does not believe that a minister should have dictatorial power over a congregation, he does insist that it is his task to advise the governing board of a church and then to help carry out what is decided. In a kind of pep talk for pastors, Schuller underscores his position:

> Leadership is to be in the hands of a living human being who is constantly thinking, constantly praying, constantly reaching out and constantly surrendering himself to the Holy Spirit of Christ. That, my big thinking, possibility thinking pastor, is YOU! Now make up your mind to be a leader. Assume your responsibility and build a great church for Jesus Christ![9]

As a corollary to this emphasis upon pastoral leadership, Schuller believes that pastors must be farsighted and willing to dig in for the long haul. Schuller learned that lesson from Raymond Lindquist, the former pastor of First Presbyterian Church in Hollywood, California, who lectured at Western Seminary when Schuller was a student. "Boys," Lindquist told the seminarians, "never take a call to a church unless you envision spending your whole life there."

Schuller tells us that he came to Garden Grove convinced that he would never leave. With a long-range interest in the church, Schuller "laid out a 40-year plan."[10]

A third emphasis is that of orienting a ministry so that it will attract the unchurched. Schuller makes no bones about the fact that he is seeking to impress the unchurched people of Orange County. "It's obvious that we are not trying to impress Christians," he says. "They would tend to be most critical of the expenditures of money we have made. They would tell us that we should give money to missions." Schuller insists that he is not really concerned about what Christians think of his ministry: he wants to catch the attention of the non-Christians and the unchurched. "We're trying to make a big, beautiful impression upon the affluent non-religious American who is riding by on this busy freeway."

Revealing that he rang 3,500 doorbells when he came to Garden Grove, Schuller claims to have discovered what impressed the unchurched in that area. They were not taken with biblical preaching, denominational labels, and organized religion. Human needs, however, were all-important. Success, sincerity, beauty, modernity, honesty, and service to the needs of the individual—these were what impressed the affluent unchurched American driving past on the Santa Ana Freeway. So one of the secrets he shares about church growth is that of learning what impresses the non-Christian, then structuring the church's ministry accordingly:

> Discover the cultural tempo of the unchurched people, and then forget what Christians may think. Forget what your denominational leaders may think. Go out and make a big inspiring impression on those non-churched people! And they'll come in.[11]

The fourth emphasis flows out of the third: don't be controversial, always stress the positive. Schuller has learned that the unchurched are looking for positive need-fulfilling experiences. A church embroiled in controversy turns them off and keeps them away. The same holds true for those who do attend church regularly. Schuller believes that one of the main reasons for the decline in membership in mainline Protestantism has been the airing of controversial issues from the pulpit. Such preaching has been offensive and divisive. Schuller argues that if a matter is controversial, it means that sincere people disagree. The pulpit is the wrong place to deal with such topics. If controversial matters need to be discussed in the church, they should be dealt with in a small classroom setting where people can fairly express their disagreements with a stated position. This is true for theological as well as political and social issues. Preaching should aim at inspiring faith rather than instilling beliefs and stirring issues. The possibility preacher must therefore be a positive preacher—inoffensive, uplifting, and affirming.[12]

The final emphasis in Schuller's approach is the necessity for having a staff ministry capable of administering a strong church program. Using the metaphor of the human body, Schuller argues that a church is able to grow when three basic body systems are functioning effectively. Evangelism is the circulatory system of the church; and because the church cannot grow unless new blood is constantly produced, evangelism must be the first priority in the church. When Schuller moved to a multiple staff at Garden Grove, he hired first a Minister of Evangelism. In turn, it was his job to "recruit, train, and motivate laymen and laywomen to be lay evangelists of the church."[13]

In a living body a skeletal system is also essential. "Converted people must become educated Christians," Schuller writes. "Education is required to furnish the skeletal structure." The second person to be added to the staff of the church was a Minister of Education, who was to "recruit, train and motivate people to be teachers in the church." Under the guidance of Kenneth Van Wyk, Garden Grove has established an impressive program of Christian education. The heart of this program is the Lay Minister's Training Center. More than 4,000 people enroll annually in 125 courses where they receive training for various forms of ministry. Called "a Seminary for the laity," the center offers courses in Bible (Bethel Bible Series), theology, psychology, counseling, teaching, and witnessing which are required for accreditation as lay ministers. Furthermore, persons who seek to become members of Garden Grove are required to take a "pastor's class" which instructs in the rudiments of the Christian faith.[14]

Finally, the growing church must have a nervous system. Having secured a Minister of Evangelism to build membership and a Minister of Education to train the new members, Schuller added a Minister of Family and Parish Life "to care for the daily needs and hurts of these members of the body." Again, the Minister of Family Parish Life has been given the task of training laypeople to do pastoral work throughout the congregation. To meet pastoral needs, the church has divided the congregation into geographical zones of eight families each. A lay pastor is responsible for the other families in his zone. This system of zoning has helped to reduce anonymity at Garden Grove, providing a network of small concern groups.[15]

So far, we have looked at the fundamental assumptions and basic emphases in Schuller's program for church growth. Now let us quickly examine the specific principles and techniques which he advocates. First, it is important to clarify terms. Schuller declares that the church must understand itself as a complex business enterprise. The retailers of religion are the local churches, who are supplied and supported by the wholesalers—the denominational head-quarters and theological seminaries. The church began to stagnate in America during the fifties and sixties because as an inefficient business it "violated the basic principles of successful retailing." Schuller explains that the postwar religion business faced issues similar to those of other marketing businesses. There was a massive move of population out of the center city to the suburbs. Wise business people followed and established shopping centers to meet the demands of the mobile multicar suburbanite. Tragically, the churches did not follow practical retailing principles and stayed downtown in the "first" churches, where there was little parking and no room to grow. The wholesalers of religion made great mistakes when they did not encourage the retailers to build "spiritual shopping centers" in the booming suburbs.[16]

Given this understanding of the church as a business enterprise, Schuller sets down his famous "seven principles of successful retailing": (1) *Accessibility.* Like all shopping centers the church must be located at major highway interchanges or major street intersections. (2) *Surplus Parking.* "The first thing you need . . . is surplus parking! Get them to park their cars, put their keys in their pockets, and you have them for a Sunday morning!" (3) *Inventory.* The church must be large enough to offer exciting programs and services and opportunities for all age groups. "Customers will go where the business has a reputation for a wide inventory range." (4) *Service.* Customers are lost unless the service is reliable. In a church, the service is provided by a trained laity. "You can't have a successful church without trained lay people." (5) *Visibility.* People need to know you are in business and what you have to offer. "You can't over-advertise." (6) *Possibility Thinking.* A growing church is committed to bold and expansive dreams which are brought into reality through prayer and persistence. "Inch by inch, anything's a cinch. All you need to get started are ideas, good ideas." (7) *Good Cash Flow.* Don't be afraid to borrow, but never allow your debits to exceed your credits.[17]

Schuller has built, then, a spiritual shopping center which has served a large number of satisfied customers. Convinced that his own success in Garden Grove is the result of applying universal principles, he urges other religious retailers to do likewise. He is certain that the business of religion will soon experience a dramatic surge of healthy growth:

> It will be a thrill to look across America in the year 2000 and see tremendous institutions in every significant city carrying out fantastic programs to heal human hearts, to fill human needs; enormous centers of human inspiration where people rally by the thousands and tens of thousands on Sundays—and gather seven days a week for spiritual and personal growth. These tremendous spiritual-growth centers; these dynamic inspiration-generating centers; these great family-development centers will be proof positive of a renewed, revitalized and resurrected institutional church.[18]

So Robert Schuller is the E. F. Hutton of the church-growth movement: when he shares the secrets of success, people cock their heads and listen. This is true first of all because he can point to the growth of his own congregation. But there is more to the Garden Grove Church than size. Nearly all who visit there come away impressed by the genuine ministry taking place throughout the congregation. The Christian education program is certainly one of the most effective in the country. And where is there to be found a more impressive lay-oriented system of evangelism and pastoral care? In addition, Garden Grove sponsors an impressive array of social and community service programs, including a counseling center, a Laubach literacy center, a day-care center, an emergency relief center, and programs for senior citizens, single and divorced persons, and prisoners, among others. Schuller must be credited for initiating and supporting a full and balanced ministry.

46

But Schuller's influence as a growth missionary is not related entirely to his remarkable but unique ministry at Garden Grove. His principles generally seem to be effective no matter where they are applied. The Institute continues to attract church leaders because it has produced thousands of satisfied customers who have spread the word that Schuller's basic principles can be successfully adapted to local circumstances. Realizing that every church will have unique forms of ministry, Schuller has designed a program rooted in principles rather than role models. As he likes to say, "There are different rules for different roles." This is certainly one reason the Institutes have persistently appealed to those who come from radically diverse theological, social, and ecclesiastical traditions.

If the proof is in the pudding, Schuller has produced a very palatable dish for the American church. Even his sharpest critics will admit that his growth principles have been effective in nurturing successful ministries. Any analysis of Schuller must begin, then, with an acknowledgment that his program has been successful in terms of membership growth. This, of course, begs the question of whether success in ministry should ultimately be measured along a standard of growth. How do we truly judge a church's success? The very issue of success, with its theological overtones, will be taken up in more detail in a later chapter.

CHAPTER IV

The Hour of Power:
Plugging into the Electronic Church

During February, 1980, Robert Schuller and his congregation celebrated the tenth anniversary of the popular "Hour of Power" television ministry. To mark the occasion, the national viewing audience was shown the videotape of a guest sermon delivered on the program years before by the late Fulton J. Sheen. It was fitting that Schuller chose to honor TV's first religious "superstar" with this rerun, for the Bishop had long been his media model and mentor. Years before, Sheen "showed all would-be broadcasters that a powerful preacher can make it on television."[1] By 1980, Schuller could legitimately claim Sheen's mantle.

Religious broadcasting began early in 1920, just two months after KDKA in Pittsburgh became the first radio station to schedule regular programs. Certain that "no harm could be done," the rector of the Calvary Episcopal Church in Pittsburgh allowed the Sunday vesper service to go over the air as an experiment. Radio and religious broadcasting boomed. Within four years, there were more than six hundred stations in America. Sixty-three of these stations were owned by churches, while a large share of the others carried regular religious broadcasts. Most of the early broadcasts were limited productions aimed at local audiences, but when the national networks became firmly established during the thirties, ministries such as "The Radio Pulpit," "The Lutheran Hour," and "The Old Fashioned Revival Hour" quickly seized this opportunity for national exposure.[2]

The development of television during the forties inaugurated another, even more significant, media revolution in America. While the first religious telecasts took place as early as Easter Sunday, 1940, when separate Protestant and Catholic services were shown, it took a decade before religious programmers truly began to understand how to use this marvelous new medium. The first successful nationally televised religious program was Bishop Sheen's "Life is Worth Living," which first went on the air in 1952. "A spell-binding speaker and a master showman," Sheen was made for television. Wearing a black cassock, with red sash, skull cap, and cape, he was visibly Catholic, but his messages, which focused upon human hurts, problems, and hopes, were decidedly nonsectarian. Millions regularly watched his primetime programs until 1957, when Cardinal Spellman moved him out of television and into the archdiocese of Rochester, New York.[3]

However short-lived, Sheen's success demonstrated the enormous potential of religious telecasting. The lesson was not lost on a group of evangelical preachers, who began to syndicate their own telecasts, buying viewing time from local stations as money became available. Employing sophisticated space-age technology to communicate a simple old-time gospel message, these persuasive evangelists eventually gained control of television's religion market. While Catholics and mainline Protestants continue to produce programs, both local and national, they have had neither the technical expertise nor the financial resources to compete with the evangelicals. So when we speak of the electronic church in America today, we are essentially referring to a number of evangelical preachers whose syndicated programs have come to dominate religious telecasting. These include Oral Roberts, who broke into television as a faith-healer but who now relies upon standard programming; Rex Humbard, whose weekly telecasts are produced from his gigantic Cathedral of Tomorrow near Akron; Jerry Falwell, whose popular "Old Time Gospel Hour" has given him a base as spokesman for the Moral Majority; Jimmy

Swaggart, the singing evangelist; Pat Robertson, who hosts the "700 Club" on his own Christian Broadcasting Network; Jim Bakker, former "700 Club" star who now hosts the "PTL Club" on his own Praise the Lord network—and Robert Schuller.[4]

The electronic church, one of its supporters has said, "has launched a revolution as dramatic as the revolution that began when Martin Luther nailed his ninety-five Theses to the cathedral door at Wittenberg."[5] An overstatement, of course. But it is true that radio and television ministries have made decisive contributions to American religious life during the twentieth century. Today, there are more than one thousand radio stations which specialize in religious programming, thirty-six television stations with full-time religious schedules, and three Christian television networks. In addition, thousands of commercial radio and television stations air syndicated televison programs. It has been estimated that these broadcasts are reaching more people in America during an average week than do all the churches combined. While such estimates have been challenged in recent studies, it is undoubtedly true that millions of Americans have, in effect, become members of the electronic church.[6]

Schuller became interested in television ministry in 1969, when he served on the committee that organized and sponsored Billy Graham's crusade in Anaheim. After the crusade, one of the Graham producers, Fred Dienart, approached Schuller and suggested televising services from the Garden Grove Community Church. Schuller's church, Dienart was convinced, would be an excellent location because it had the kind of visual movement—fountains, doors, trees, cars, and other things—which would make for good television. Moreover, he was certain that the charismatic Schuller would make an ideal lead personality for a weekly program. Schuller remembers becoming excited about the possibility, envisioning a spectacular color telecast framed with the serene natural setting of trees, flowers, and fountains.[7]

But when Dienart later came back with a report indicating that it would cost around $400,000 a year to produce the program, the usually ebullient Schuller became an instant impossibility thinker. He explained to Graham's producer that his congregation had just completed an extensive fund-raising program to buy ten acres of land next to the church for additional parking, and that the church board was about to ask the congregation to increase the budget by more than $100,000.

Dienart would not give up. He called Schuller a few weeks later and told him that it would take just $200,000 to get the service on the air and that the challenge of the project should be presented directly to the congregation. "Why don't you and I give God a chance to make this decision?" suggested Dienart. "*If the decision is no, let God make it.* Next Sunday, have your people come to church and lay the plan before them. Let them respond."

So Schuller, on the model of Gideon, decided to "lay out the fleece." He and Dienart made a quiet covenant with God. If $200,000 in pledges were forthcoming in the following two weeks, the worship service would go on the air in January of 1970.

Before the first test-Sunday, the congregation was notified by mail that "Dr. Schuller was about to make one of the most important decisions of his life" and that he would ask the members of the congregation to direct him. Pledge cards were found in the bulletins. On the first Sunday morning, 1,100 families pledged $186,000 toward the project. A week later the pledges totalled more than $200,000, and the television ministry was off the ground. In telling the story of this fund-raising, Schuller reminds us that even he had underestimated the power of possibility thinking. "God had taught me a lesson. He taught me that I was 'too-little-a-thinker.' "[8]

Having been given God's green light, the church proceeded to form a corporation called The Robert Schuller TeleVangelism Association, Incorporated. Stuart Erhlich, a layman in the church, was hired to administer the project, and Frank Bos, treasurer and business executive of the church, was designated the financial officer of the new corporation so that Schuller would be "personally immune from financial criticism in the handling, receiving and discharging of funds." Dienart's Walter Bennett Agency, which handled the Billy Graham television specials, was chosen to produce the "Hour of Power." Since the agency had initially presented Schuller with the challenge, it was natural for them to take over production of the new program. After a few years, however, MASCOM, an in-house advertising agency, was set up to produce the "Hour of Power."[9]

Having built an administrative framework for the television ministry and having received enough pledge money to begin operations, Schuller announced that the first service would be videotaped on the third Sunday in January, 1970, and that the actual telecast would begin the first Sunday in February. All was not clear sailing. A week before taping was to begin, word came that new lights and transformers would have to be installed in the church sanctuary immediately at a cost of $10,000. This crisis was averted at the last minute when a tithing couple, whom Schuller had never met, walked into his office and presented him with a $10,000 check for use as he saw fit. Schuller remembers receiving the check with tears in his eyes. "It was God's way of saying, 'Schuller, this is My project. Stay out of My way. Only be willing to think big, believe big and pray big—and big things will happen!' "[10]

The lights were installed and the taping began as

scheduled. But the project quickly ran into another problem—congregational resistance. When it became apparent that the "Hour of Power" would become a reality, an extensive campaign was launched to prepare the congregation for what would be involved in taping a service: "they would have to see beyond themselves and into the 'reaching' effect of the ministry."

Arvella tells us that there was great support and tremendous enthusiasm for the project when it was announced, but that a strong backlash of criticism and disappointment soon developed. The people, she explains, were just not ready "for the cameras, the crew that came in smoking, dressed in 'grubbies,' and just generally out of tune with the congregation."[11] Most of the criticism quickly abated as the "Hour of Power" gained more control over the taping. Today the crews are much less obtrusive and much more in tune with the congregation. Then, too, the congregation has simply adjusted to the unavoidable distractions. In fact, some who attend the Sunday morning services have certainly been lured there, in part, by the opportunity of participating in a media event. After all, they may even be caught on camera! As one visitor put it a few years ago: "It's the only place around where you can see a church service and the production of a television program at the same time."[12]

After more than a decade of broadcasting, most of the production wrinkles have been ironed out. In fact, "Hour of Power" is generally considered one of the best produced programs on religious television. Mike Nason, executive producer of "Hour of Power," claims that one of the problems with Christian television has been the tendency to "mimeograph and staple Jesus." Taking exception to those who feel that low budgets and amateur programming reflect true Christ-like humility, Nason insists that "Christ must be presented in a *FIRST CLASS* manner. *Hour of Power* is successful because of Dr. Schuller's original commitment to be FIRST CLASS in everything he presents."

Convinced that Christ must be presented in full color to compete with every other option confronting the viewer, "Hour of Power" has hired a highly respected professional video recording company, Pacific Video of Los Angeles, to do the taping. Actually, an arrangement with Pacific Video now allows "Hour of Power" to hire its own production crew—in effect, to tape its own services, with Pacific Video providing the equipment. The cameramen, recording personnel, and stage manager work directly for the executive producer.[13]

"Hour of Power" was originally tested on a West Coast station, where it caught on quickly. Confident that the program would do well in the large urban markets, MASCOM began to buy telecast time in New York, Philadelphia, and Chicago. It appears on more than 165 stations throughout the United States, Canada, and Australia. According to recent figures supplied by both the Arbitron and the Neilson television rating services, "Hour of Power" has a weekly audience of over two and a half million Americans, making it the most popular of all the weekly religious telecasts.[14] Another study by Arbitron indicates that Schuller's program attracts a larger audience in the Eastern section of the country than any of the other media ministries. This is probably because the music and messages on "Hour of Power" are stylistically less attuned to the Bible-belt. Schuller has long been popular in the Midwest and is becoming more popular in the South; he has also done well in the West, especially in California. Like other television ministers, Schuller is watched by more women than men and by a high percentage of older people. Arbitron has determined that between two-thirds and three-quarters of all syndicated religious telecasts have viewers of over fifty years old and that two-thirds of these are women.[15]

Legally separate from the Garden Grove church and housed in a modern corporate-style building across the street from the Crystal Cathedral, Schuller's television ministry is self-supporting. The annual budget of twenty-five million dollars is small when compared with the other programs which make up the electronic church. Falwell, for instance, takes in as much as seventy-five million dollars a year from his telecasts. "Hour of Power" is supported entirely by donations sent by viewers. Generally, Schuller has refrained from direct solicitation for funds, but when a viewer is invited by an announcer (often a member of the Schuller family) to send for copies of sermons, books, or possibility-thinking hardware (a mustard seed, an inch-by-inch ruler, golden pendants, etc.—all of which Schuller prefers to call "think-its" rather than trinkets), she or he is also invited to make a donation. Many do just that. On the average, "Hour of Power" receives 30,000-40,000 letters a week and more than half contain money to be used in support of the ministry.[16] Schuller has discovered that offering gifts has become a necessary gambit financially. Carl Wallace, director of administration for "Hour of Power" explains:

> You can't just preach the gospel and wait for the money to come in. . . . It doesn't happen that way. You've got to offer some incentive for people to communicate with you. The minute we stop offering gifts, our revenues go down dramatically.[17]

The "Hour of Power" offices include a large "reader's room" where each weekday sixty-five to seventy volunteers (out of a pool of 250-300) handle the thousands of letters addressed to Dr. Schuller. Many of these letters, of course, request one of the gifts which are being offered, but a good percentage also seek guidance and support from the TV pastor who speaks always of health, happiness, and success. The volunteers remove the donations and then sort the letters according to the nature of help sought by the writer. From that point on the computerized typewriter takes over. A suitable form letter primed with a positive word from Dr. Schuller and an uplifting scriptural passage is quickly sent to the viewer under Schuller's signature—computerized pastoral care for one of the more than 800,000 persons on his mailing list.

Schuller often points out that the success of "Hour of Power" is due in great part to the fact that he is broadcasting rather than "narrow-casting."[18] As a mission to the un-churched, the show has been choreographed in every way to attract and hold the attention of the viewer. Schuller is acutely aware that the viewer is free to switch channels. He perceives his audience with their hands on the channel selec-tor: his challenge is to keep them tuned.

Actually, except for editing and other technical flour-ishes, "Hour of Power" is a televised version of a regular worship service at the Crystal Cathedral. It is fair to say that most of the components of this service were hammered out by Schuller at Garden Grove long before he began a tele-vision ministry. Interested in attracting those who were turned off by institutional services, Schuller learned early on that people need to be entertained: "99% of all Sunday morning services are a drag and a bore"—dull and uninspir-ing hymns, whole chapters of Scripture, dead spaces for meditation, and long guilt-producing sermons. All of this gives people a negative impression of the church:

> They feel that if they want to laugh they have to go to a nightclub. They have the impression that the church is a giant put down. It is not the place to go if they want to feel good when they leave.[19]

So people who attend the Crystal Cathedral or tune in the "Hour of Power" are entertained, allowed to laugh and to think happy, positive thoughts. Timing and pace are impeccable; the "dead spots" in most worship services are eliminated and the show seems to move freely and spontaneously.

Music plays a major role in setting the tone of "Hour of Power." While the musical program may vary, each service normally contains two short congregational hymns, two choir anthems, and two numbers sung or played by guest musicians. The music is screened to fit the basic religious perspectives of the show. Arvella tells us that "it all has to be positive, uplifting; it has to appeal to a wide scope of audience."[20]

Since "Hour of Power" has gained national prominence, the program has been besieged by musicians wishing to appear on the show. It has been possible, then, to be quite selective, and guest musicians are usually unpaid. Again, the guest numbers are screened for properly positive lyrics and suitable tempo. Congregational hymns follow a consistent pattern as well. They must be positive, singable, and nonsexist. They must also be noninstitutional—which rules out hymns like "The Church's One Foundation" and "Rise Up, O Church of God." "If the purpose of *Hour of Power* were to reach and inspire other churches," Arvella has said, "we'd use those, but our purpose is to reach the unchurched person." Arvella also admits that she rewrites the lyrics of certain hymns to give them more acceptable wording.[21] Furthermore, in line with the positive approach, hymns of penitence and confession are never chosen. To confess sins, even in music, would be appropriate only for committed Christians, and since many viewers have not made such a commitment, they should not be manipulated through a confession which would reinforce a negative self-image, and contribute to an atmosphere of defeat and impossibility thinking.

One of the stock features of "Hour of Power" has been the weekly appearance of a celebrity guest. When he began the show, Schuller invited only the occasional guest, but when letters indicated that viewers identified the programs with the guests who had appeared, Schuller realized the importance of the guest spot. In accord with one of his basic principles, that "people listen to their peers and not through their ears," guests fall into various categories: movie, TV, and musical personalities (Mickey Rooney, B. J. Thomas); sports heroes (Steve Garvey and Tommy John), evangelical giants (Billy Graham, Oral Roberts, Corrie Ten Boom, Chuck Colson); business entrepreneurs and success motivators (Richard DeVos of Amway, Wilbert Eichenberger of the Growth Institute). Periodically, noncelebrities are invited as well, people who have overcome obstacles through positive persistence and strong belief. Arvella describes the most effective pulpit guests: "Those who have a story of faith to share—something they've done physically that's 'impossible,' a problem they've handled with God's help, or somebody who is just a joyful and successful person."[22]

Through music, guest spots, gift offers, and impressive camera shots of flowers, fountains, and the glass Cathedral itself, the "Hour of Power" moves toward a climax— Schuller's own message of possibility thinking. The Scripture has already been introduced and read by Robert A. Schuller, the star's son and the heir apparent of Schuller's ministry, who remains a visible part of the "Hour of Power" while pastoring his own congregation in San Juan Capistrano, a city located about forty miles south of Garden Grove. Invariably the passage which is chosen provides a scriptural base for a positive message.

After an inspiring choir anthem, the camera focuses upon Schuller himself, who stands alone behind a long marble pulpit. Dressed in an impressive grey doctoral academic robe, his silver hair perfectly coiffed, Schuller commands respect while at the same time emitting genuine warmth. He does not have a booming oratorical voice, but his speech is strong and persuasive and he uses it with dramatic intensity—whispering one moment and shouting the next. His gestures are animated but not mechanical and are normally synchronized with his voice. Like Fulton Sheen, Schuller possesses a dramatic flair which attracts and holds his audience. And through some televisual chemistry, he is able to gain immediate rapport with his listeners. It is as if he has let each one of us in on something very personal.

An extremely effective communicator, Schuller has learned that success in television depends as much upon style as upon substance. Few of his messages are literary masterpieces when converted into print. Prepared to be delivered with some spontaneity, and never read, they are not especially smooth or poetic. But, in his own rather casual and off-handed manner, Schuller is a persuasive and inspirational pulpiteer.

In an interview with the editors of *The Wittenburg Door,* Schuller indicated that he is successful as a preacher because he is intentionally inspirational. Arguing that preaching ultimately fails unless it inspires, he went on to develop a two-pronged rationale for this approach. The primary goal of the preacher should be to "create an experience" rather than to preach sermons. In Schuller's lexicon a sermon is an automatic turn-off for the unchurched audience. Most people, he claims, identify sermons as judgmental put-downs by a self-conscious expert who has placed himself on a moral pedestal:

> A guy who sits up there with a clerical collar may not say it, but he really thinks he's a little bit better than those guys down in the pew. He may claim to believe in the priesthood of believers. That's what he professes. Really, he thinks he knows a lot more about it. He studied Greek and Hebrew and they didn't. He went to an accredited theological seminary. He knows more about it than they do. That's preaching a sermon. If you have that attitude,

you will create, you will emit emotional vibrations that do not build spiritual relationships between pulpit and pew. When you witness, you create an experience. When you preach sermons, you produce polarizations.[23]

The second principle of inspirational speaking is that the message should begin from the heart and not from the head. Sermons can be persuasive only when they testify to the personal experiences of the preacher. Schuller believes that he is persuasive because he is sincere and that he is sincere because he speaks only about those matters which have affected his own life. If you are faithful to the principle of preaching from your heart rather than from your head, you will avoid those topics which have little personal meaning. Schuller put it this way:

> If you ever hear me preaching a sermon against adultery, you know what my problem is. If you hear me preach a sermon where I'm so enthusiastic about the coming of Jesus Christ, when He's going to come, and what's going to come before Him, you know that's where I am heartwise. It so happens that I'm not hung up on either of those areas, so I've never preached a sermon on either one.[24]

Schuller is convinced that witnessing is the most effective form of communication. Hence, his liberal use of true-to-life success stories and personal examples.

Schuller further contends that sermons should be need-oriented and positive rather than controversial. He admits that he avoids touching upon issues of controversy but claims that his mission is that of healing rather than raising issues which produce negativity and division. He sees his role as that of pastor rather than prophet.[25]

The standard possibility-thinking message is often capped with a broad invitation for the audience to turn their lives over to Christ. This is portrayed as the final solution to the human predicament. It is this practice which has helped to identify Schuller as a member of the broad evangelical movement that has been surging in America since the late sixties. But Schuller's sawdust trail is wide, relatively easy to traverse, and filled with positive gain. Well aware that too much talk about commitment to Christ will send his audience to the channel selector, the altar call, such as it is, is given at the end of the message, just before the show is concluded. This is clearly part of his overall plan:

> One of my non-Christian friends said, "I love to listen to you because you don't get to Jesus Christ until the end, and when you do, I can turn it off." Don't you see? That's my strategy.[26]

With Schuller the medium and the message converge. Few communicators are as effective at reaching through the television screen and touching viewers where they live. And having come to understand their hopes, fears, and anxieties, Schuller has learned to apply the subtle techniques of mass communication. One can isolate at least five.

First, Schuller communicates on a very immediate and personal level. The message is invariably addressed to the second person singular. He is speaking directly to us. "How do you see yourself today? What are your strengths? What are your weaknesses? What are your personality assets? What are your personality liabilities? What is your future going to be like?"

It is difficult to evade such personal questions. Like all effective preachers, Schuller understands that second person personal pronouns are hotter and more emotion-laden than the third person personal pronouns. He pursues us relentlessly. The messages are never removed or dispassionate; they zero right into our emotions. Again, change starts with our heart, not with our head.

Second, Schuller uses the personal interest story. He has learned that people are more interested in personalities than in philosophizing, as any survey of the newstand will quickly demonstrate. Schuller has certainly capitalized on the success story: rags into riches, failure into success, mountains into miracles. These, of course, are as American as hot dogs, apple pie, and Horatio Alger. And no one tells the story better than Schuller.

Third, Schuller appeals to well-known authorities to support his program of possibility thinking. He quotes extensively from experts, especially psychologists, like Viktor Frankl. Schuller also appeals to the biblical writers. He is a textual rather than expository preacher, and the texts chosen always have a positive outlook and therefore allow him to expand upon his favorite theme.

Fourth, Schuller relies on a steady stream of aphorisms, epigrams, and slogans—frequently alliterative and usually banal: "Every problem is a possibility"; "Inch by inch, everything's a cinch"; "Meter by meter, life is sweeter"; "If you fail to plan you are planning to fail"; "Aim at nothing and you'll succeed"; "There is no gain without pain"; and "Turn your scars into stars." Before we snicker at these verbal potions, let us admit that we do remember them. Schuller is not interested in winning the Pulitzer Prize for literature: he wants to get his message across.

And fifth, Schuller is the master of the method and technique. Invariably prudential, his messages belong to the "how-to" genre. Short on philosophy and long on method, Schuller's sermons appeal to Americans because we are desperately interested in accomplishments, in results. We are therefore told in arresting detail how to change our negative self-image, how to turn stress into strength, how to save our marriage, how to gain peace of mind, how to build a bigger and better church. Schuller is the mass therapist dispensing practical formulas for success, happiness, and health. His popularity is due in part to the fact that he supplies practical solutions for people who face real problems.

63

The electronic church has come under mounting criticism from those who have become alarmed by its spreading power and influence. Most of the critics have been mainline Protestants who have felt comfortable with neither the style nor the substance of the evangelical-dominated media ministries. A number of evangelicals, however, have joined in raising some tough questions about the electronic church. Among the concerns expressed are these: (1) the electronic church is gaining supporters and funds at the expense of the local church; (2) money raised through "hucksterism" is being misused and mismanaged by the stars of the media ministry; (3) electronic preachers are gathering a right-wing political constituency; and (4) the gospel proclaimed by media ministers is dangerously abbreviated and woefully misdirected.[27]

Some of the observers of the electronic church have noted that Schuller is the only primetime preacher who stands within the tradition of mainline Protestantism rather than Bible-belt evangelicalism.[28] He is, therefore, given special treatment in an analysis of the media movement. Wishing to disassociate himself from the fundamentalist overtones of certain TV ministries, Schuller prefers to call himself a minister from the mainline denomination of Norman Vincent Peale. While it is certainly true that Schuller is less overtly evangelical than some of the other television preachers, it is a mistake to remove him altogether from the evangelical orbit. In music and message, the "Hour of Power" is subtly permeated with the flavor of evangelicalism. A bridge between evangelicalism and mainline Protestantism, Schuller's ministry deserves to be scrutinized as a legitimate representative of the electronic church.

Schuller would dispute the claim that "Hour of Power" is draining members and money from the local church, and recent studies tend to support him on this point.[28a] Indeed, he would deny that his television following should even be understood as members of an electronic church. "What you see on television is not a church," he explains. "Don't call that a church. Call it emotional therapy, or a ministry or ecclesiastical activity, but don't call it a church."[29]

And just as Schuller denies that there is such a thing as a television church, he denies that anyone can be a television pastor. Despite the illusions of intimacy which Schuller's warm style and "personal" letters suggest, he admits that there is a vast gap between the television ministry and the local pastorate: "I can't baptize your children, comfort your sick or bury your dead." When people join his own congregation at Garden Grove, he tells his television viewers:

> Wherever you live, not far from you there is a church. Look for it. Shop around. You're going to find a church which is like ours. Maybe it won't be big like ours or have the same architecture, but don't be fooled by the structure. Be attracted by the Spirit!

Furthermore, Schuller has revealed that his favorite letters are those which say, in effect, "I no longer watch your television program. I did what you said; I am now going to church."[30]

It is difficult to assess whether people are staying home from church on Sunday mornings to watch "Hour of Power." Those concerned that the electronic church has been pulling money and people from the local churches may be overreacting. In fact, supporters of the media ministries argue that those watching television ministers have even increased their church attendance and their giving. In general, the drop-off in attendance at mainline churches during the past two decades cannot fairly be blamed on the primetime preachers. There are other reasons for such decline. Schuller claims that "Hour of Power" is a missionary venture intended to feed the local church. Whether this is actually true can be settled only by the kind of empirical evidence that is not yet available.[31]

Schuller likes to think that he is in a class by himself when it comes to the ethical question of whether television ministers have misused or mismanaged funds. He is probably right. The financial operations of the "Hour of Power" have been made public from the beginning, and there has never been a hint that donations have been illegally used or that Schuller has benefited personally from the funds. Schuller receives no pay from his television ministry. In fact, for several years he has accepted no salary from the Garden Grove congregation—only housing allowances and car expenses. Essentially his income is derived from speaking fees and publication royalties. While he lives comfortably with a home in Garden Grove and a cabin in the mountains (which he is in the process of turning over to the church), Schuller has not lived ostentatiously. The charges of financial indiscretion hounding some of the media ministers have not appeared at Schuller's doorstep—in part, he claims, because he is protected by an institutional safeguard:

> The difference between me and those others is that my church is part of a mainline denomination. I'm accountable to the board of the Reformed Church in America. I turn in a financial report every year. I can be called on the carpet any time. I wouldn't want it any other way.[32]

When John Mariani wrote a hard-hitting piece for the *Saturday Review* called "Television Evangelism: Milking the Flock," he more or less exempted Schuller from suspicion of hucksterism. Schuller could not be put "in the same alms box" as some of the other television evangelists.[33] Schuller himself likes to point out that he doesn't pitch for money on television, and that his fund-raising strategy is morally circumspect. And it is certainly true that "Hour of Power" is less blatant in soliciting funds than many of the other big-time TV ministries. But on the air or through the mail, Schuller never fails to remind his supporters that he needs their donations. There is nothing illegal or deceptive about his approach, but one may wonder whether many vulnerable and undiscriminating people could have found better use for the ten or twenty dollars sent to Garden Grove. Much advertising, after all, is the art of getting people to buy something they do not really need.

Those who are convinced that the electronic church has helped to galvanize a right-wing political constituency are undoubtedly correct. Jerry Falwell and other television evangelists have certainly contributed to the politicization of evangelicals since the 1980 national elections. Schuller, in contrast, has taken little or no active part in this socioreligious crusade. While his self-help message might be interpreted by some as oriented toward social, economic, and political conservatism, Schuller has assiduously avoided being caught in the religious stampede to the political right. In fact, in concert with his belief that the pulpit should be positive, therapeutic, and noncontroversial, Schuller has avoided speaking out on any public matters. This avoidance of the issues has brought criticism from both the left and the right. But Schuller has refused to move an inch in the direction of politicizing his ministry.

The fourth and final concern about the electronic church is that it produces a simplified and distorted version of the gospel. It is certainly true that television religion provides simple solutions to human problems, and much of this has to do with the medium itself. Because television does not handle complicated material very well, communication must be done simply and quickly. Furthermore, people use television to be entertained and reinforced rather than challenged or scolded. So, programs which do not make people feel good about themselves are not going to be successful. Jeffrey Hadden and Charles Swann tell us that television evangelists have shaped their messages to conform to "the logic of television":

> TV preachers must say what they have to say quickly and simply, and it must be entertaining and supportive of viewers' values and sense of self-worth.

Hadden and Swann suggest that these media requirements have resulted in three basic themes in television preaching. (1) The world and the self must be understood in unambiguous terms. The impression of absolute certainty must be communicated in spiritual, moral, and ethical matters. (2) An enormous benefit will be derived from a positive approach to life. (3) It is all right to look out for ourselves: selfishness is not a sin.[34]

When it comes to his media preaching, Schuller conforms perfectly to the above-mentioned paradigm. His messages are understandable, entertaining, positive, and selforiented. It is little wonder that he has found success as a televangelist—he tells people exactly what they want to hear in the manner which pleases them most. He doesn't insult people by telling them they are sinners, and he doesn't tell them that it is wrong to pursue personal dreams of success and happiness. In fact, possibility thinking seems to be the perfect vehicle for self-fulfillment.

It would be tempting to conclude that Schuller's gospel has been shaped by the logic of television. That is simply not the case. Aware that the messages delivered on "Hour of Power" are simplified treatments of Christian faith, he defends himself with the claim that he is attempting to reach the unchurched. He understands himself to be a preevangelist who feeds the multitudes milk because the meat of the gospel would prove indigestible.

But beyond that, Schuller is truly convinced that his message of possibility thinking *is* the pathway of the gospel—through faith we *do* achieve self-fulfillment. The television version of the gospel is simplified, to be sure, but according to Schuller, it faithfully represents Christian truth. In the next two chapters we will take a closer look at Schuller's understanding of the gospel.

CHAPTER V

Possibility Thinking

The trademark of Schuller's religious enterprise is "possibility thinking." This upbeat expression, which so compactly epitomizes the thrust of his ministry, has served to give Schuller a special identity. And like most patented trademarks, this one is ubiquitous: it is neatly stamped onto nearly everything related to Schuller and his twenty-two-acre spiritual shopping center in Garden Grove. Three of his popular books bear the trademark: *Move Ahead With Possibility Thinking, Peace of Mind Through Possibility Thinking,* and *The Greatest Possibility Thinker Who Ever Lived.*[1] And if one visits the Garden Grove campus, he or she can buy these books at the Possibility Thinker's Bookstore. Viewers of the "Hour of Power" are encouraged to join the Possibility Thinker's Club, whose members, of course, subscribe to the "Ten Commandments of Possibility Thinking" and "The Possibility Thinker's Creed." In addition, a "Possibility Thinker's Game" has been made available (through Scrabble Brand Products) for those wanting a little practice at overcoming life's difficulties.

Nearly all of Schuller's books begin with the promise of a wonderful new life through possibility thinking. When we turn to the first page of *Reach Out for New Life,* we are greeted with these enticing words: "Welcome Reader! You are about to enter the great way of living that we call Possibility Thinking." The introduction to *You Can Become the Person You Want to Be* offers the same fulfillment:

> Are you disappointed, discouraged and discontented with your level of success? Are you secretly dissatisfied with your present status? Do you want to become a better

and more beautiful person than you are today? Would you like to be able to really learn how to be proud of yourself and still not lose genuine humility? Then start dreaming! It's possible! You can become the person you've always wanted to be!

How? There is a KEY—there is a SECRET—there is a WAY—to turn impossible dreams into fantastic accomplishments. I call it *Possibility Thinking*.[2]

Interested as we all are in becoming better and more beautiful people, we read on. And Schuller proceeds with illustrative detail to share his surefire formulas for success.

What is possibility thinking? In one of his recent books, Schuller defines possibility thinking as "that mental attitude which assumes that any objective that is noble, admirable, or beautiful can be realized even if it appears to be impossible." Elsewhere, Schuller has suggested that what he calls possibility thinking others call "faith."[3] But this would not be an explicit or parochial faith—faith in God or faith in Christ—but the belief that all things are possible. The faith that moves mountains here is the faith which believes that mountains can be moved.

Possibility thinking is of course a slightly refurbished version of the positive thinking philosophy ably espoused by Norman Vincent Peale. While Schuller has been reluctant to compare his brand of positive religion with Peale's he has nonetheless acknowledged an intellectual debt to his good friend from New York. Peale has even been asked to endorse and preface some of Schuller's early books.[4] When Schuller grabbed hold of Peale's coattails back in the drive-in ministry days, he apparently grabbed hold of Peale's positive-thinking messages as well.

Let us try to isolate the essential elements in the process of possibility thinking. Schuller begins by assuming that most of us are basically dissatisfied with our lives and want something better. Unless we come to grips with this vague discontent and dissatisfaction, however, we will never become motivated to begin to turn our lives around. This is why Schuller begins so many of his sermons and books with probing personal questions:

> How would you describe your life in emotional terms? Are you happy-go-lucky? Or uptight and tense? . . . Do you find your enthusiasm turning into despondency? . . . Do you find negative emotions and upsetting and unsettling thoughts dominating your mind most of the time? Is your life today less than satisfying and do you often feel mysteriously unhappy?[5]
>
> Are you really content to live the rest of your life the way you are living right now? If your answer is "Yes, I'm content," then you have a problem. You are selling your life too cheaply, and that's a sin. But if your answer is "No, I'm not content to live my life the way it is today," then you have some great, even fantastic, possibilities ahead of you.[6]

Essentially, Schuller starts us along the road to possibility thinking by helping to lay bare those frustrations, anxieties, and miseries which contribute to our dissatisfaction and sense of failure. He begins with our problems, which is his way of reminding us of our sinful condition without insulting us, of pointing out the results of sin in our daily lives without demeaning us. While the old-time evangelists softened people to the gospel by elaborating their sins, Schuller softens people for possibility thinking by reminding them of their discontent. And what he offers is a cure, a technique for changing lives. But like the potential convert in the revival tent, the potential possibility thinker must come to the point of acknowledging discontent and desiring a better life.

As we contemplate better, more successful lives for ourselves, we are activated by a divine booster. Schuller informs us that God wants us to be happier, healthier, more fulfilled. Those impossible dreams, grand plans, and glamorous goals are to be viewed not as frivolous or self-centered but as divinely inspired. In fact, God has a marvelous plan for our lives which we must discover and begin to work through. In a sense, success is a matter of fitting into God's groove.

Not only does God have a plan for our lives, which he will carry through to completion, but we are worthy of this divine confidence. After all, we are God's invention; we have been made for greatness. To underscore this point, Schuller quotes the proud ghetto youth who refused to allow his environment to crush his sense of self-worth: "My name is Johnny Jones. And I know I'm black. And I know I'm beautiful, because God don't make no junk." He also recalls a remark attributed to Ethel Waters, the great black singer: "God don't sponsor flops."[7] So we are encouraged to believe in ourselves because God does, and to dream the impossible dream because it is truly part of God's will. The divine challenge is placed squarely before us:

> It's happening all around you today. Disadvantaged, defected, discouraged people are learning how to change their lives, their futures, their destinies. Now it's your turn to stop failing and start succeeding. Discover the better idea God has for your life. You are God's idea and God only dreams up beautiful ideas. He's expecting great things from you. Cooperate! Believe in yourself, NOW, and draw the possibilities out of your being.[8]

Once we have acknowledged that we are not content with our lives, that we desire change, and that we believe God has a plan for our lives, we are told to pray for and think positively about the goal we wish to attain. Possibility thinking is a technique for obtaining whatever worthy goal we seek. We are told how to become wealthy, how to make our marriage work, how to obtain a happy family life, how to overcome physical handicaps, how to secure peace of mind, how to rid ourselves of tension, how to raise our children, how to earn higher grades in school. As far as Schuller is concerned, these specifics all spell success.

What does Schuller mean by success? A crucial term in the lexicon of possibility thinking, success appears to have two shades of meaning. On the one hand, it is simply achievement, reaching one's "predetermined objective."[9] This, of course, is the common designation, and Schuller's sermons and books are filled with illustrations of those who have been high achievers in American society. We are inspired by baseball players who became World Series heroes, doctors who struggled through medical school to become famous brain surgeons, and businessmen who built empires through positive principles.

Schuller is obviously enamored of the super successes of our world, but not simply because they stand at the top of the heap in wealth and power and prestige. More impressed by achievement than by status, Schuller warns that there is no standardized scale with which to measure success. Since success must be understood as individual achievement—the realization of predetermined goals—one person's success may be another's failure.[10]

Measuring success in this way, Schuller is able to describe Jesus Christ as a great success. One of Schuller's sermons, later published as a book, proclaims Jesus Christ as "the greatest possibility thinker that ever lived" because he overcame seemingly insurmountable obstacles to achieve his life's purpose. In building the ultimate "scars-to-stars" story, Schuller portrays Jesus as an ostensible misfit who seemed to have nothing going for him. He was

a member of a despised minority,
a citizen of an occupied country,
a nobody as far as the Romans were concerned,
a joke to the occupying power,
a nuisance to His fellow Jews.

And as if these impediments were not enough, Jesus is further described as poor, uneducated, untravelled, uncultured, with no social connections and no functioning organization.[11] But in the end, Schuller tells us, Jesus was a huge success because he achieved "predetermined measurable, manageable objectives." First, Christ was successful because he carried out his plan to live and die as a sacrificial savior. And second, he successfully employed the strategy of the cross to achieve another objective, that of spreading the gospel to the ends of the earth. Jesus was the greatest possibility thinker of all time because he accomplished everything he had set out to accomplish.[12]

While Schuller relates success to achievement, he employs another, more distinctly religious definition which seems to innoculate his possibility thinking against the charge that is essentially materialistic and self-serving. In *The Peak to Peek Principle*, Schuller suggests that "success is building self-esteem in yourself and others through sacrificial service to God and to your fellow human beings."[13]

This definition reveals two significant principles in Schuller's system. First, notice that high self-esteem is the pivot for success. Schuller has written that "all supersuccessful people know that self-esteem is life's highest value." He warns us, therefore, against gaining the whole world while losing our self-respect. "You may accumulate riches, fame, and honors, but unless you achieve tremendous self-esteem in the process, all that the world calls success becomes ashes in your hands."

Second, notice that while Schuller links success to service, what we do for others may be a byproduct of our search for self-esteem. Schuller urges us to follow our own path to success convinced that, along the way, our success will benefit others. "It's impossible to succeed," Schuller writes, "without being a servant to someone." Schuller wants us to succeed, and he wants us to serve others, but if building self-esteem is "both the motive and the measure of success,"[14] then service becomes a fruit of success, or a necessary condition for maintaining high esteem.

Possibility thinking rests upon the conviction that human beings are free to control their own destinies, to actualize their own lives. Schuller emphasizes that neither our environment nor our genetic make-up holds us prisoners. Even when we are faced with physical constraints, our minds are still free to react in a way which is nonprogrammed and individual.

Schuller has illustrated this point by relating a death-camp discovery of Viktor Frankl during World War II. When he faced his Nazi accusers, Frankl was stripped naked, seemingly left without one shred of human dignity. It was then that Frankl discovered the key to self-esteem. The Nazis, he concluded, could control everything except how he might respond to their atrocities. He could die with dignity because he was in control of his response to external forces.[15] Schuller urges his readers to believe that they are existentially free:

> It's not what happens to you in life that makes the difference. It is how you react to each circumstance you encounter that determines the results! Each human being in the same situation has the possibilities of choosing how they will react—either positively or negatively.[16]

With this understanding of human freedom, Schuller places the burden of failure squarely on the shoulders of the individual. "Now let me tell you why you fail," he announces to readers of *Reach Out for New Life*. "You fail because you deliberately, knowingly, and willingly choose to fail!"[17] As responsible beings we are not allowed to blame our failures on the circumstances of race, age, sex, education, class, and financial resources. People must stop playing the game of "Let's Pick Out the Villain." To those who blame their woes on the capitalistic system, Schuller counters: "In spite of its faults, our free enterprise system—more than any other in the world—allows you the freedom to choose to try to become anything your heart desires." To those who suggest that the Establishment is putting them down, Schuller responds: "Sorry! That's a sweeping, negative generalization that would never stand up in the court of reality. The hundreds of thousands of disadvantaged people who are making great strides today in our Establishment turn this argument into an excuse." In another context, Schuller reminds those who are victims of racial prejudice that there are exceptional individuals who succeed despite this problem. "If you live in a community where racial prejudice does, in fact, exist," Schuller writes, "don't use this as an excuse to keep from trying. Use it as a challenge to hurdle over the obstacle!"[18]

By kicking the crutches from those who blame their failures upon circumstances, Schuller does not mean to put people down. His message is intended to achieve precisely the opposite. Every person has the capacity and the freedom to choose to overcome these obstacles to success. Schuller glories in the potential of the individual. Possibility thinking is a message of human autonomy and actualization.

If it is true that we are endowed with the capacity to succeed, why are we so often ridden by failure? Schuller has a ready answer to this pivotal question. We fail because we do not believe in ourselves, because we possess a negative self-image. Unless we can gain a positive self-image we will never have the self-confidence necessary to achieve success. While we will deal with his "theology of self-esteem" in the following chapter, we must understand at this point that Schuller believes this negative self-image to be humankind's basic problem, a very part of original sin, a kind of sickness of the human condition which obstructs health, happiness, and achievement. The entire process of possibility thinking revolves around the need to boost self-esteem.

Essentially Schuller is a mass therapist who writes prescriptions for sick egos. We have already noted that he seeks to inspire us with the message that we are inherently worthy and created for greatness because we are inventions of God. If we can believe that God "don't make no junk" and that God "don't sponsor flops," we will "suddenly rise to a self-confidence" which will give us "power to transcend obstacles, prejudices, handicaps, and set-backs." But Schuller also knows that we carry burdens of guilt and anxiety which inhibit positive self-esteem and destroy positive potential. And of course, as a Christian minister, Schuller proposes that the good news of Christ is that he removes our guilt and thereby restores our self-esteem. Here is how Schuller summarizes this doctrine of redemption:

> Why does God want to forgive us? Because in forgiving us he helps us to love ourselves. And only when we love ourselves will we dare to believe that we can and will become the sons of God we were created to be.[19]

As a means of their achieving self-esteem, Schuller urges his readers and listeners to give their lives to Jesus Christ. Schuller's altar call is unlike that of most hard-sell evangelists. There is no humiliating call for repentance, no threat of damnation. Still, God's way to the good life depends upon a commitment to Christ. "I know," Schuller tells the readers of *Discover Your Possibilities*,

> that ultimately you will never be the person you want to be, you will never solve the problems you've never solved before, until you make a real deep commitment to God and to Jesus Christ. And that's how your total life can be renewed and your mind and your life transformed.

Schuller goes on to warn the listener that to turn off Christ is to turn off "the magic key" to success through possibility thinking.[20]

In most of his early books and sermons Schuller actually devotes relatively little time to explaining the theological principles we have noted. Like most of the secular proponents of positive thinking, Schuller concentrates upon the practical task of conditioning our attitudes. He is convinced that our minds control our destinies, that our attitudes shape our lives. We are what we think we are. Time and time again he has stated that there are no personal or cultural obstacles which cannot be overcome. Thus, one can hardly overstate the role attitudinal psychology plays in Schuller's system: "Power, success and achievement will come to you anywhere you are if your attitude is right."[21] Or as Zig Ziglar, another positive thinker, puts it: "It's not your aptitude but your attitude which determines altitude."

The great villain of possibility thinking is the negative thought or emotion. Schuller puts great stress upon exorcising negative thoughts from our minds, because like weeds they crowd out the positive thoughts and inhibit the mind's concentration upon success. A great believer in the power of words, Schuller tells us not even to utter the ten-letter negative word "impossible." In fact, we are warned that we should *"never verbalize a negative emotion,"* for to do so would confuse our subconscious. "You will give your doubts legs to stand on. You will support your fears and misgivings. Before you know it your dreams will be trampled under a herd of goal-smashing impossibility thoughts." And when we feel a negative emotion coming on, we should never say, "I'm tired, or angry, or hurt," for that would strengthen and empower the negative force. To verbalize such negatives would mean "giving in and surrendering your will to an enemy." That would mean defeat. The best means to confront and overcome the negative emotion is to counter-attack it with a positive emotion. Schuller explains by using a common metaphor:

The only sensible way to fight weeds is to plant thick, healthy grass. The only successful way to destroy a negative emotion is to verbalize a positive statement. You counterattack the invading negative emotion by shooting the positive counterpart.[22]

"The most dangerous and destructive force on earth," says Schuller, is the Negative Thinking Expert. Because he is an expert we tend to listen uncritically to what he has to say. "With the authoritarian hauteur of a brilliant intellectual snob" the Negative Thinking Expert will enumerate all the reasons why an idea is "unrealistic, beyond credibility, ridiculous, unthinkable, and impossible." Such a person is inevitably a hindrance to progress, development, creativity, and advanced thinking.[23]

The Impossibility Thinker is the Negative Thinking Expert's first cousin. Schuller often uses this creature as a foil for the Possibility Thinker. The Impossibility Thinker is someone who "immediately, impulsively, instinctively, and impetuously" torpedoes positive suggestions. Afflicted with the "impossibility complex," these sorry people are "problem imaginators, failure predictors, trouble visualizers, obstacle-envisioners, exaggerated-cost estimators . . . worry creators, optimism deflators, confidence squelchers" who bury positive ideas and smash impossible dreams. Schuller, who himself never flinched from tackling tremendous tasks, has made it his life's ambition to convert these negative thinkers into exponents of creative possibilities. Convinced that the Impossibility Thinker can become a Possibility Thinker, Schuller has even proposed an "eight-step treatment for the impossibility complex," a treatment which depends upon a daily massage for the negative self-image.[24]

Having told us how to combat disabling negativity, Schuller is now prepared to show us how to arm ourselves with enabling positive attitudes. Remember, Schuller believes that our attitudes control our actions—positive thoughts produce a positive self-image which produces positive results.

Certain that success is predicated upon positive attitudes, Schuller has suggested a number of mind-conditioning techniques in his sermons and books. We have already discussed one such technique: neutralizing negative emotions with a positive counterpart. Reading Schuller, one discerns at least four other mind-conditioners: visualization, meditation, affirmation, and repetition.

In *Move Ahead With Possibility Thinking,* Schuller devotes an entire chapter to the technique of "imagineering," the act of visualizing the goal one wishes to achieve. The chapter title is instructive: "Let Your Imagination Release Your Imprisoned Possibilities." Schuller is convinced that we can transform our personality through positive imagination. "Visualize yourself as a relaxed, charming, confident, poised, smiling person. Firmly hold this mental image of yourself and you will become this kind of person." Our imagination can even transform our physical appearance. If we truly wish to become friendly, cheerful, and attractive people, we need only practice positive imagination as a daily ritual. Our "smile muscles" will become so strong that our face will be transformed. "Beauty," Schuller insists, "is mind-deep." We are as beautiful or as ugly as we think we are.[25]

As a personal testimony to the power of imagineering, Schuller tells us that he actually lost forty pounds of unsightly fat through positive imagination. "I drew a mental image of the kind of physique I wanted and held that vision before me constantly." The secret of imagineering is that when we "draw a clear mental picture and get a sharp mental definition" of what we really want, we release surges of enthusiasm. This enthusiasm produces ambition, and with ambition we begin to "pray, plan, and plug." Soon

our project is off the ground.[26] It's all a matter of conditioning the mind. Schuller has taken his cue from the writer
of Proverbs: "As a man thinketh in his heart, so is he."

In *Peace of Mind Through Possibility Thinking*, Schuller
endorses meditation, long practiced in Asian cultures, as
a technique for overcoming the distractions of the conscious
mind. He suggests that T.M. (Transcendental Meditation)
and other common meditational practices, while not anti-
Christian, are essentially non-Christian. For this reason, he
advocates "the meditation which Christ practiced," which
he calls PTM, or Possibility Thinking Meditation. PTM, of
course, is really the traditional practice of prayer, but
Schuller has given it a special twist. The purpose of PTM
is "to reach the state of relaxation where you can be released
from negative tensions that block the positive flow of creative
ideas—even the very voice and Spirit of God." "Meaning-
less mantras repeated over and over," says Schuller, "will
never be as effective as Christian meditation which brings
Jesus Christ's love into our daily lives." With Christ in our
lives, we won't need another "guru." Schuller goes on to
lay out the five steps for reflective Possibility Thinking
Meditation:

(1) Neutralize your mind. ("Imagine your brain in neu-
tral, simply and quietly purring and humming, con-
centrating on nothing but the soft, quiet, neutralizing
vibrating mental hum.")
(2) Harmonize. ("You line up your mind with God.")
(3) Sterilize. ("Relax and allow God to draw out the
mental poisons.")
(4) Tranquilize. ("If you feel you would benefit from a
'mantra,' take the I am's of Jesus Christ and repeat
them softly, chanting, humming, affirming His presence and peace within you as you recite His
promises.")
(5) Visualize. ("Move your mind now to meditate upon
peaceful scenes.")[27]

Schuller also suggests that we "harness the super-power of positive affirmations." Similar, in many respects, to the form of psycho-cybernetic conditioning popularized by Maxwell Maltz, these affirmations are considered impor-tant because they can bend our minds toward a positive end. In various books, Schuller has listed sets of positive affir-mations similar to these cited in *Reach Out for New Life:*

> Affirmation No. 1: "I affirm that I will never be defeated, because I will never quit."
> Affirmation No. 2: "I affirm that God expects me to be tough-minded, and I am."
> Affirmation No. 3: "I affirm that God is stronger and bigger than my problem."
> Affirmation No. 4: "I affirm that God has people all lined up waiting to help me at the right time, in the right place, and they will show up; people I don't even know and have never met."
> Affirmation No. 5: "I affirm that God will turn my worst times into my best times and my scars into stars."
> Affirmation No. 6: "I affirm that I can never fall away from God's love."
> Affirmation No. 7: "I affirm that if I'm totally dedicated I'll eventually win."[28]

The most familiar affirmation in Schuller's arsenal of mind-conditioners is his "Possibility Thinker's Creed," a hallmark of the Schuller phenomenon which is found on pendants and posters throughout America. Practitioners of possibility thinking are advised that daily recitation of this creed will help to overcome obstacles to success.

> When faced with a mountain
> I will never quit
> I will keep on striving
> until I
> climb over,
> find a pass through,
> tunnel underneath,
> or simply stay and

turn the mountain
into a gold mine!
With God's help!²⁹

Finally, Schuller advises that the repetition of positive words or verses will inspire us to achieve our goals—demonstrating his confidence in the power of words and thoughts. Closely related to the affirmation technique, repetition amounts to a form of autosuggestion. Indeed, according to Schuller, we can talk ourselves into almost any attitude. In *Move Ahead* he instructs readers to repeat a set of affirmations out loud. The list includes phrases such as "I can do great things" and "I have great possibilities deep inside me." Schuller admits that the task may be very difficult for some. "You will feel like a hypocrite, a braggart, and a liar. But read—OUT LOUD—then repeat again and again LOUDER—these powerful affirmations." Convinced that positive repetition can produce transformed minds, Schuller encourages us to keep at it. "Your biggest problem," he tells us, "will be to believe it deeply enough to try it long enough and loud enough to dehypnotize yourself from the mesmerizing power of your impossibility thinking." Schuller tells how Dr. Daniel Poling, a well-known minister in New York City, overcame doubts and negative thoughts by repeating three times upon arising every morning, "I believe, I believe, I believe." Schuller adds his own "mantra" to Dr. Poling's: "I can, I can, I can."³⁰

In general, Schuller advocates the exercise of memorizing and repeating positive Scripture verses. It is common practice in the Schuller household, he tells us, for the family to take such a spiritual vitamin each day while gathered around the breakfast table. A short Bible verse is memorized—short so that it can easily be held in the mind all day. Schuller prescribes many such vitamins throughout his writings.

Here's a sampling from *Move Ahead*:

Luke 1:37—"With God nothing shall be impossible."

Mark 10:27—"With men it is impossible, but not with God."

Matthew 19:26—"But with God all things are possible."

Mark 10:27—"For with God all things are possible."

Luke 18:27—"The things which are impossible with men are possible with God."

Mark 9:23—"If you can believe all things are possible to him who believes."

Mark 14:36—"Father, all things are possible."

Matthew 17:20—"If you have faith as a grain of mustard seed, you can say to this mountain move, and nothing shall be impossible."[31]

Schuller guarantees that when people begin to use these mind-conditioning techniques they will become possibility thinkers. He does not, however, guarantee immediate and automatic success. The road to achievement is filled with obstacles which must be overcome with patience, persistence, and prayer. It may take a long while to achieve the impossible—mountains are not moved overnight. After all, Madame Curie performed nearly 400 experiments before she discovered radium; the beautiful temples of Baalbek took 200 years to be built; and many of the magnificent cathedrals in Europe took 400 years to complete. The key to success is often the ability to wait out adversity. In commending patience—and persistence—Schuller reminds his readers that God's timing is much better than our own. Therefore, we should not become discouraged. "God's delays are not God's denials."[32] The seven affirmations we have cited are to be supplemented with a set of "God-is-able" Bible verses, such as "He is able to keep you from falling and slipping away" (Jude 2) and "He is able to do far more abundantly than we ask or think" (Ephesians 3:20). Martin Niemoller survived the horrors of the Nazi concentration camp at Dachau by hanging on when everything appeared hopeless.

"You are much stronger than you think you are. . . ,"
Schuller quotes Niemoller as saying, "*if God is dwelling in
your life.*"[33]

Schuller is well aware of the roadblocks to success
which possibility thinkers must face, but he is convinced
that these obstacles have been placed there for a purpose.
He is certain that life is made richer because of the strug-
gles which are faced and overcome. In *Reach Out for New
Life* he states ten principles which relate directly to this
theme:

1. There is no growth without separation.
2. There is no meaning in life without challenge.
3. There is no conversion without crises.
4. There is no way of helping people without hurting
   them.
5. There is no adventure without risk.
6. There are no great movements without great issues.
7. There can be no life without clouds.
8. One person's need is another person's opportunity.
9. There is no creativity without conflict.
10. There is no resurrection without death.

Citing these universal principles as evidence, Schuller explains that "we can say with scientific and spiritual integrity
that there is a light behind every shadow." In fact, he is
willing to claim that these shadows are actually providen-
tial, for they indicate that "God has a design for every
difficulty."[34]

Schuller disagrees with those critics who have dismissed possibility thinking as shallow Pollyanna. He claims
that he is profoundly aware of the real pain and misery people must endure. But behind every problem he discerns a
purpose and a promise. Rather than allowing genuine problems to stymie us, we must turn problems into possibilities,
obstacles into opportunities, scars into stars. A few years
ago, Schuller's teenaged daughter Carol was in a motorcy-

cle accident which resulted in the amputation of one of her legs. Not long after the surgery, she told her father that she was going to turn her pain into gain by devoting her life to others who had lost limbs. "I've got to look at what I have left," said this young possibility thinker who saw the light behind the shadow, "not at what I've lost."[35]

Schuller is absolutely convinced that those who practice possibility thinking will achieve success. The proof, he would say, is in the pudding. And over the years he has gathered testimonies from thousands of people who claim to have turned their lives around with his positive approach. His sermons and books are replete with such testimonies; the "Hour of Power" has introduced a stream of guests who have told inspiring stories of achievement. Only the hard-boiled cynic would deny that Schuller's positive process has brought thousands of people hope, happiness, peace of mind, and a sense of achievement. To be sure, it would be difficult to verify some of these claims with scientific rigor. But from nearly every angle of investigation, possibility thinking seems to be effective. But why? How does it work?

Schuller seems to be aware of three operative components in the process of possibility thinking. First, he has isolated a physiological component. This fascinating assessment is found in the introduction of *You Can Become the Person You Want to Be*:

> Here's how it works, when a person begins to believe it just might be possible, somehow, someway, somewhere, someday—then in that magic moment of Possibility Thinking three miracles occur: 1) Opportunity-spotting brain cells activate! 2) Problem-solving brain cells come to life! 3) Determination-energizing chemicals are released into the bloodstream.

Schuller has suggested that if we simply think of and repeat the word "possible," we would "begin to release creative brain cells from their invisible prison of subconscious defensive mechanisms.''[36] While these statements may seem bizarre to many of us, Schuller could argue that scientists have been making important new discoveries in this field, linking thoughts and emotions to bio-chemical functions and reactions.[37]

Obviously, the physiological component is inextricably intertwined with the psychological. We have already noted that much of the possibility-thinking process is taken up with techniques of mind-conditioning and thought-control. It is fair to say that Schuller is a mass therapist who advocates a form of self-actualization which is similar, in many respects, to that advocated by humanistic psychologists. At any rate, Schuller would not shrink from the charge that he has psychologized the gospel, for he is convinced that the gospel and such psychologies are in no essential conflict. He has even stated that biblical truth and psychological truth are essentially the same.[38]

We may not conclude, however, that Schuller merely baptizes psychological method with the holy water of pious platitudes and Bible verses—that he is a kind of Zig Ziglar or Dale Carnegie of the pulpit. This is not a fair reading of possibility thinking. Schuller adds a religious component which is generally missing from the messages of the secular positive thinkers. As we have already noted, he believes that negative thinkers must come to terms with God before they can become successful. And this is not a matter merely of acknowledging a cosmic force or believing in providence, but of actually making a personal commitment to Christ. Schuller tells his listeners and readers that they will never become the persons they want to be unless they acknowledge that Christ sets them free from guilt and anxiety. Furthermore, Schuller's emphasis upon prayer moves him beyond those who advocate a secular gospel of success. Again and again he has stressed that ''Prayer + Possibility Thinking = Success.''[39]

Schuller is well aware that many people will accept the psychological component of possibility thinking while rejecting the spiritual. But he insists that Christ is the way to the good life. After imploring the readers of *Discover Your Possibilities* to make a commitment to Christ, he offers this instructive analysis of motives:

> You listen to me when I talk about psychology and psychiatry and when I tell you my funny little stories. But when I start zeroing in to say "My friend, have you ever received Jesus Christ into your life? Have you ever turned your life over to Jesus Christ and to God Almighty?" that's when you turn me off. You get flighty like a bird. Well, I dare you right now to turn me off. Because you may be turning off the magic key. When your commitments are right, you're ready to work on your priorities.[40]

One of Schuller's harshest critics has dismissed possibility thinking as "pop psychology and mythical physiology" wrapped up into "infantile formulas for successful living."[41] Such an assessment is simplistic. Possibility thinking may indeed be a blend of psychology and physiology, but it is certainly more than that: it is anchored to an apparently evangelical understanding of new life in Christ. This helps us to understand why, in this evangelical era, Schuller has been endorsed and embraced by Billy Graham and other evangelical leaders.

Schuller's success with possibility thinking is related, at least in part, to the fact that he has synthesized two strains of popular American culture. On the one hand, he promotes a religious message which is rooted in evangelicalism. On the other hand, he advocates a psychological method which stresses self-actualization. An "equilibristic"[42] thinker who has consistently sought to synchronize the sacred and secular, Schuller has balanced evangelism and psychology within his process of possibility thinking. All of this begs further analysis of the theology of self-esteem, the true fulcrum of Schuller's system.

CHAPTER VI

The Theology of Self-Esteem

Schuller is convinced that his message has mainly been misunderstood and misinterpreted by the American theological establishment. Usually imperturbable, he becomes agitated by those "sophisticated professors" who tell people that "Schuller is ridiculous" and his message "shallow."[1] While he could retort simply that his ministry is directed at the masses rather than at academia, Schuller does not want to be so easily dismissed as a popular religionist. He is, he insists, a sound theologian who deserves a full and fair hearing from the community of scholars.[2]

Throughout most of his career, Schuller admits, he has had little time to flesh out a complete systematic theology, and he avers that this is one reason the professionals have failed to take him seriously. Certain that his ministry has been based from the start upon solid theological principles, Schuller has often lamented that he has been so busy meeting the immediate spiritual needs of those he has been called to help that he has not had the chance carefully to elaborate those principles. During the mid-seventies, Schuller compared himself to an emergency-room doctor who had made many important therapeutic discoveries, which, given his hectic schedule, he has not had time to share adequately:

> You see some things are working because you've developed the skill, reputation, and expertise in working in this emergency room, but you don't have time to put down some of the things you've learned. Some of the new techniques. Meanwhile, the professors of the medical school don't bother to ask you because you're just working in the emergency room of the Orange County Hospital.[3]

Now, after more than thirty years of successful practice, Schuller has published a book which seeks to tell the medical school professors what medicine is all about. *Self-Esteem: The New Reformation* is the first of a multivolume project which Schuller once estimated would take him more than ten years to complete.[4] While this work contains little that Schuller had not already suggested or outlined in earlier sermons, articles, and books, it is the first of his books that tries to deal with theological questions systematically.

Written in that popular style which characterizes all of Schuller's publications, the book is certainly not a typical theological tome. In fact, most of the work is decidedly devotional and inspirational. Still, *Self-Esteem* is clearly not meant to be just another motivational tract or success manual. Schuller is targeting this book not at the "Hour of Power" audience but at the leaders of the American church—the pastors, lay leaders, and denominational bureaucrats who might be interested in a new and positive theological foundation upon which to build revitalized and successful congregations.[5] In the end, Schuller's theological system appeals far less to the established doctors of theology than to those who, like Schuller, have been laboring in the religious emergency rooms all over America, binding up those broken and hurting people who have found the church irrelevant to their lives.

The theology of self-esteem is, above all, a theology of mission. In the introduction to *Self-Esteem*, Schuller acknowledges that his basic approach to theological questions has been determined by his lifelong ministry to unbelievers. As one who has seen his calling as that of a missionary trying to reach the unchurched, Schuller has found it necessary to begin with "human needs" rather than with theocentric matter. It is folly, he contends, to expect non-Christians to be interested in biblical pronouncements and theological assertions. The unbeliever will take notice,

Schuller submits, only when we "demonstrate genuine concern about their needs and honestly care about their human hurts."[6]

Schuller's call for a "new reformation" is based upon his conviction that the classical theologies of the past cannot be effectively transmitted in today's secularized culture. There was a time when "God-talk" was an appropriate enterprise for Christians. Luther and Calvin, for instance, could "think theocentrically" because everyone belonged to the church and understood biblical and theological categories. "The reformers didn't have to impress the unchurched," Schuller suggests, and therefore found it unnecessary to employ the human-needs approach. But times have changed. The once secure superstructure of Christendom has collapsed, and the church of our era has fallen sharply "in power, membership, and influence." Indeed, this very decline came about because the church placed "theocentric communications above the meeting of the deeper emotional and spiritual needs of humanity." Having turned inward and speaking a language which the initiated alone could understand, the church itself is responsible, in large part, for the fact that Christianity has become listless and ineffectual in the Western world.[7]

So, having diagnosed the contemporary church to be seriously ill, Schuller announces that what it needs, above all, is "a new theological reformation." It is Doctor Schuller's prognosis that without such a reformation—without a radical shift in thought from a theocentric to an anthropocentric approach—"the Christian church as the authentic body of Christ may not survive." And here is the tough prescription he writes for the ailing patient: "The church must be willing to die as a church and be born again as a mission."[8]

But Schuller professes to be essentially optimistic about the future. As a churchman and theologian within the Reformed tradition, Schuller states that he "must believe that it is possible for the church to exist even though it may be in serious error in substance, strategy, style, or spirit." So, convinced that nothing less than a reformation will save the church, he has given himself to this holy cause. At times he seems to see himself in the shadow of Martin Luther himself, who in the face of criticism and opposition was haunted with the question, "Am I alone right and is all the rest of the church wrong?"[9]

This latter-day Luther has steeled himself for the opposition his new reformation will encounter from those whose feet remain firmly planted in the sixteenth century. We are living, Schuller believes, in the "last days of the Reactionary Age in Church history"—an era dominated by the theocentric approach of the Protestant Reformation. Indeed, Schuller is certain that we are already witnessing "the birth of a new Age of Mission," which will be centered in the human-needs approach. Expressing a unique brand of millennial expectation, Schuller suggests that the 2000th birthday of Christ will be identified by future church historians as the pivotal date in the rebirth of Christianity.[10]

The following description and analysis of Schuller's theological program has been drawn from various articles and certain chapters of his earlier books as well as from *Self-Esteem: The New Reformation*. While theologically more comprehensive than any of his other writings, *Self-Esteem* is not offered as a definitive systematic treatment of his theology. Moreover, most of the theological principles elaborated here had already been set forth in other writings, often with succinctness and clarity.

The theology of self-esteem begins with an examination of the human condition. In preparing his diagnosis, Schuller first examines the symptoms of that general human malaise Kierkegaard called "a sickness unto death." Here he relies on the analysis of Robert Ardrey:

96

> I feel a restiveness in man, a dissatisfaction of a univer-
> sal sort. The average human being, as I judge it, is
> uneasy. He is like a man who is hungry, gets up at night,
> opens the refrigerator door and doesn't exactly see what
> he wants because he doesn't know what he wants. He
> closes the door and goes back to bed.[11]

Not knowing what we really want, we go through life "with
a strange inner hunger unsatisfied." Or, to take another
of Schuller's metaphors, we are like people who have holi-
days but do not know what to do or where to go; by the
time they decide, it's too late. Or we are like the little boy
who can't decide how to spend his money at the toy store
and when he finally buys a whistle, breaks down in tears
halfway home becaue he has already grown tired of the
sound.[12]

Having diagnosed these universal symptoms, Schuller
poses a crucial question: "What is the deepest need of
human beings?" What is that gnawing hunger, that restive
ness which afflicts the human spirit? Schuller believes that
the church has failed to deal realistically and honestly with
this basic question. Through the centuries, the church has
assumed that every person's basic need was "salvation from
sin"; it therefore held out "hope for forgiveness" as the
ultimate answer. Schuller does not argue with the correct-
ness of this traditional assessment, but he does suggest that
it is a "casual or cavalier" approach for those non-Christians
who cannot comprehend this exclusive theological language.
By not adequately posing the all-important question of the
ultimate nature and will of the human being, "theologians
have abandoned an essentially theological question to other
disciplines and professions." It is Schuller's conviction that
during the last century social scientists, especially the
psychologists and psychiatrists, have most faithfully pursued the question of the deepest human needs.[13] So, in pur-
suing that question himself, he elaborates the conclusions

97

of various social scientists and then uses these conclusions as a means for clarifying his own.

Is the will for pleasure the basic driving force in life? Sigmund Freud, we are informed, believed that it is. But Schuller notes that people forsake physical pleasure in favor of work, love, religion, and war. "Man," he observes, "craves something much deeper than pleasure." What of the will to power? Psychiatrist Alfred Adler held that the lust for power was humanity's basic drive. But Schuller dismisses this theory on the ground that power alone cannot produce respect. Like the will to pleasure, the will to power is simply one of those "swirling streams on the surface of a river" which distract people from discovering the major currents underneath. Other observers of the human condition have, in Schuller's judgment, come closer to locating our basic need. When Abraham Maslow speaks of the will to self-actualization, Rollo May of the will to create, Erich Fromm of the will to love, and Viktor Frankl of the will to meaning, each has identified "a strong subsurface current in man" but none, Schuller surmises, has identified the basic force.[14]

Schuller suggests that the ultimate drive of human nature, the deepest of all needs, is "the awareness that we are worthy persons." This "will to dignity" is described as "the irreducible, psychological, and spiritual nucleus around which the life of the human soul revolves and evolves."[15] All of the other drives—for pleasure, power, creativity, love, self-actualization, meaning—"are symptoms, expressions or attempts to fulfill the primal need for personal dignity." The drive-wheel of human existence is self-esteem. "Even the will to discover meaning," says Schuller, is nothing but "an expression of the will to achieve self-esteem. . . . Even meaning loses meaning unless it fulfills our self-esteem." Schuller concludes his diagnosis with this summary statement: "Man is a pleasure-seeking, power-seeking, love-seeking, meaning-seeking, creativity-seeking animal because he is first and foremost a dignity-seeking creature."[16]

Because self-esteem is the cornerstone of Schuller's theological system, it is imperative that we understand precisely what it means. Originally, Schuller used the term "self-love," but he tells us that he abaondoned it because it was so often misunderstood as selfishness or self-will. Furthermore, he dropped the term for the simple reason that "the people who do not have it are offended by it."[17] "Self-esteem" is less likely to be misinterpreted, but Schuller still takes pains to define it carefully as "a crowning sense of self-worth . . . an ennobling emotion of self-respect . . . a divine awareness of personal dignity." Eager to set the record straight, he insists that self-esteem is not arrogance, for this form of egotism is actually "a breezy symptom of a trembling insecurity." Likewise, self-esteem is not narcissism, which, like arrogance, is "a symptom of the pitiful lack" of self-respect. Above all, Schuller wants to dissociate self-esteem from self-will, which he describes as "an aggressive expression of the inner lack of self-assurance."[18]

Having diagnosed the basic human malaise as an abiding need for self-worth, Schuller proceeds to tell us why we possess such a strong will to self-love. He probes this issue by relating a conversation he once had with Viktor Frankl. He asked Frankl why, of all the living organisms which emerged from "a slimy amoeba in a swampy pool," the human being evolved with a craving for self-worth and self-esteem? We are told that Frankl was unable to answer the question. Schuller, however, had a ready answer: humans are dignity seeking beings because God has created them that way. Going to the creation story in Genesis for support, Schuller stresses that mankind was made for greatness. In fact, the first humans were created in the very image of God, just a little lower than the angels. As children of God, "divine dignity" is "our emotional birthright." As an act of confidence, God placed mankind in charge of the created order. Endowed with dignity, authority, and freedom, humanity was "a supreme display incarnate. . . . the star of God's creation!"[19]

While acknowledging the fallenness of humanity, Schuller insists that "the Fatherhood of God is built into our subconsciousness" and that through a "universal religious 'instinct' " we are emotionally aware of our divine heritage.[20] The primal God-given urge for dignity has been dulled, but not destroyed through the centuries:

> The urge for greatness, the compulsion to create, the passion for excellence, the desire for recognition, the discontent with imperfection, the demand for personal freedom, the need to give and receive love, even the desire to rule and dominate—all originate with our ancestral divine heritage when God made the human being to be great, glorious and perfectly proud.[21]

If Schuller's doctrine of creation explains why we are driven by a craving for dignity and self-worth, his doctrine of the Fall explains why this drive is so often submerged beneath feelings of self-doubt and inadequacy. While he is usually reluctant to dwell upon the negative components of the Christian faith, and therefore loathe to focus on human sinfulness, Schuller has set forth a doctrine of the Fall and it has a pivotal role in his theological system.

Schuller seems to have adopted a literalistic interpretation of the story of the Fall as found in the third chapter of Genesis. At no point does he deny the historical reality of Adam, Eve, Satan, or the "first sin." But if Schuller is essentially unadventuresome in his exegesis of the Genesis text itself, he is quite daring and innovative in his interpretation of the consequences of the Fall.

Following the biblical account, Schuller tells us that Adam (he does not mention Eve) was created without sin,

but "like the child of a famous father who may be tempted
to rebel against his father's overpowering shadow," Adam
asserted himself and sinned against God:

> When that happened . . . [Adam] became separated from
> God. Feeling guilty, he hid in the bushes to avoid being
> caught by the Almighty. . . . That is what "original sin"
> is all about. It means that we are all born detached from
> a relationship with God, and consequently suffer from
> birth with a terribly weak and insecure ego.[22]

Notice that Schuller makes a critical distinction between the
"first sin" of rebellion and the "original sin" which resulted
in "a terribly weak and insecure ego." Adam, born without
sin, freely chose to rebel. He knew better. The descendants
of Adam, however, did not have a choice. They were "born
in the bushes, in hiding." They are not so much rebels as
cowering victims of Adam's sin of rebellion. In fact, Schuller
tells us that we can rightfully give Adam a sermon on sin—
"he deserves it"—but that we should not lay a guilt trip
on Adam's children and his children's children. After all,
they are not really responsible for their sinful predicament.[23]

And so the core of original sin is being born with a
negative self-image, an "inherited inferiority complex"; it
is not in itself rebellion against God. Adam's sin has left
us stripped of our self-assurance—"so emotionally starved
that we become vain, rebellious and self-serving."[24] Pride,
then, is a consequence of our loss of self-esteem and not
the cause of our woeful human condition.

Schuller is aware that his doctrine of sin, which he
offers as "scientific" and "scriptural,"[25] conflicts with those
theological traditions which have identified rebellious pride
as humankind's basic sin—the "original sin" which all of
us share with our spiritual parents, Adam and Eve. In a
panel discussion on self-love that was later published in *Eternity* magazine, one of the participants suggested that

Augustine was correct in his conviction that the trouble with man boiled down to the fact that he loves himself too much, not too little. Schuller immediately responded, "St. Augustine was wrong on that point. I don't accept that. If your interpretation is correct, he didn't have the advantage of some of the information available to us today." Schuller went on to note that willful pride is the opposite of true self-esteem; it is "the ultimate reflection of a person who has not come to terms with himself."[26]

Schuller does not deny that humanity is afflicted by the sin of pride, but he insists that this destructive self-centeredness is merely a symptom of the ultimate human problem, inadequate self-esteem. To illustrate this point, Schuller offers us the image of a cross-section of a golf ball. On the outside, the ball is covered with hard dimpled plastic. Likewise, from a surface examination we learn that human beings commit proud and rebellious actions against God. But that rebellion is "merely the outer cover, the externality of sin." Beneath the plastic cover are layers and layers of tightly stretched rubber bands. These rubber bands represent "the anxieties, fears, and negative emotions that finally present a face that appears to be angry, mean, rebellious." The webbings of rubber bands are wrapped around a small rubber pea located at the very center of the golf ball. Here at the hidden core, all human beings are afflicted with a negative self-image. The classical theologians, we are told, make the mistake of identifying the surface of rebellion as the essential nature of sin, because they have failed, in their analysis, to cut through to the core of the human condition.[27]

While Schuller has elaborated a unique interpretation of original sin as a negative self-image, he actually spends little time focusing directly upon sin in his ministry. There are three reasons for this. First, Schuller believes that people are fully aware that they are weak and sinful. No need to verbalize what is painfully self-evident. "Deep down in our hearts," says Schuller, "we all sense our imperfections and guilt." Second, and more important, Schuller does not say much about sin because he is afraid that such talk will simply reinforce a negative self-image. He has, therefore, counseled pastors to avoid talking about sin with their parishioners:

> Don't tell them they're sinners. They'll believe you—and you'll reinforce this self-image! You'll set this negative impression in their minds and their conduct will only prove how right you were.[28]

Third, Schuller avoids talk about sin because he believes that it is an ineffective means of reaching non-Christians.

At the Crystal Cathedral Schuller, of course, practices what he preaches. Not only are his messages sanitized of sin, but many of the hymns have been altered to avoid demeaning phrases. Nor is there any regular confession of sin in the morning services. That would be like a physician's prescribing whiskey for an alcoholic.

Schuller's strategy of evangelism is directly linked to his understanding of sin. Being born in the bushes with the curse of low self-esteem, people have become distrustful and afraid of God. Their rebellion against God, then, is really a defense mechanism thrown up to protect them from a threatening relationship. To approach non-Christians with the message that their rebellious pride is the essence of their sin will simply push them away from God. "When we say that original sin is rebellion against God, that's shallow theology, and it is dangerous theology because it produces a destructive strategy of evangelism."[29] If the basic problem with nonbelievers is a low self-image, it is also insulting and slanderous to tell them that they are wretched sinners. Such an approach violates their self-respect. Even the worst sinner, Schuller insists, deserves to be treated with dignity. "He's not a shack; he's a cathedral. He may be a cracked cathedral with the windows destroyed; he may be in ruins because of his rebellion, but he's still a cathedral because he was created in the image of God."[30]

In this respect, Schuller believes that he is merely following the example of Jesus Christ. If Jesus were on television today, Schuller is convinced, his ministry to the masses would be positive and nonjudgmental. Never would he say, "You are sinners. Repent and be baptized."

> Jesus never called any person a sinner! He recognized the reality of sin. He recognized the fact that all persons were sinners, *but* to convert them, he didn't use the strategy of calling them sinners![31]

Jesus, then, was the greatest possibility thinker who ever lived. He consistently affirmed the individual's "undeveloped, undiscovered and unclaimed positive possibilities!" Jesus didn't tell people that they were bad—not even the prostitutes and tax collectors. Instead he told bad people that they were beautiful, and "eventually the 'bad' began to believe they were 'good' and the belief became a self-fulfilling prophecy." Jesus was the Great Person Promoter who sought "to help every person achieve redemption from an inherent negative self-image to a positive self-image."[32]

Schuller often tells the story of *Man from La Mancha*, the popular play adapted from Cervantes' *Don Quixote*. It is Don Quixote's fervent belief that the wench Aldonza is actually a lady of great gentleness and dignity. While first she scorns Don Quixote as insincere, she eventually accepts his image of her as her own. And thus, because Don Quixote believed in her, she comes to see herself as the worthy Dulcinea. "She has been saved from self-hate and has been taught self-love," observes Schuller. "She was truly born again."[33]

While Christ is the only one who can completely remove the burden of the sin of a negative self-image, each of us must be Christ-like in projecting the positive in our relationships with others. Convinced that people become what they are expected to become, Schuller implores us to tell persons what we wish them to be rather than what they are. After all, "I am not what I think I am. I am not what you think I am. *I am what I think you think I am.*" While it may seem trite, Schuller's little benediction, "God loves you and so do I" is a consistent summary of this theological-psychological principle. Schuller insists that the benediction is more than a catchy slogan. "It is a proud, positive proclamation of the Cross—the vertical and horizontal intersection of a relationship with God and a relationship with those around me."[34]

Schuller's doctrine of redemption follows naturally from his doctrine of sin. Born in the bushes with a shattered self-image, we must be coaxed out of the shadows of insecurity and have our lost dignity restored. "Somehow," writes Schuller, "we must be born again and emerge trusting and enthused about the kind of persons we can be with the help of God."[35]

Schuller recognizes that because we are born with a negative self-image, we are destined to commit numerous sins against God and our neighbors for which we bear a great burden of personal guilt. Remember that the rubber core of the golf ball was wrapped by tightly stretched rubber bands of anxiety, tension, fear, worry, and guilt, and that these remained just beneath the surface of outward acts of rebellion and pride. Schuller defines guilt as "the negative emotion experienced by a 'conscience-mind' that passes a personal moral judgment upon itself." It is important to note here that Schuller is accepting an almost Kantian notion of imperative moral law. Individuals tend naturally to sense that they fail to measure up to some inherent moral standard. Schuller tells us that guilt is a great imposter which

masks itself behind fear, doubt, hostility, grief, loneliness—
but that no matter how hard we work at covering up our
feelings of guilt, our subconscious guilt remains. In Freud-
ian language Schuller warns, "You can chloroform the con-
science, but you cannot anesthetize the subconscious."[36]
Our guilt will remain with us until we feel forgiven.
And because forgiveness cannot be offered except by the
one who has been offended by our sins, God alone can
remove our deep-seated guilt. When divine forgiveness is
experienced, we will be free from those insecurities and self-
doubts that have inhibited self-assurance and inner pride.
But there is one more hitch in this process of redemption.
Forgiveness cannot come without acknowledgment of guilt
and turning from sin in a process traditionally known as
repentance.

Schuller does not often speak of repentance, but he
does acknowledge that it plays a role in redemption. In one
of his books, Schuller approvingly quotes psychiatrist Karl
Menninger:

> Nothing will bring healing quicker to people than repen-
> tance. They're sinners and they know it. They're respon-
> sible for their guilt. They'll never be healthy until they
> confess and repent before God.[37]

Schuller agrees that repentance is important, but he insists
that it must never be a process of self-abuse and self-
abrogation. Claiming that Jesus never asked people to grovel
in the dust before he lifted them up, Schuller suggests that
many contemporary Christians have failed to follow their
Master's example. He compares some orthodox Christian
leaders to the Pharisees whom Jesus did berate because
"under the guise of authoritarian religion, they destroyed
man's sense of self-affection and self-worth." In a reference
perhaps to the repressive and judgmental strain of Christianity which Schuller may himself have endured as a

youngster, he writes, "Perhaps nothing destroys one's sense of self-respect more than the finger-pointing, wrist-snapping, fist-shaking religious authority which claims to speak in the name of God."[38]

ˣSchuller chides those negative-thinking theologians who have failed "to interpret repentance as a positive creative force." He reminds us that *metanoia*, the Greek word for repentance, means "the turning of one's life from sin to the Lordship of Christ." Those persons, overwrought by a "mortification mentality," who debase, humiliate, and negate themselves before God, betray the divine dignity which is their rightful heritage.[39] We are not asked to cower or grovel before the Almighty, but simply to confess our sins and ask forgiveness. God is not "a vengeful, fearful being," but a gracious and forgiving Father. When we come to his Son seeking forgiveness, Jesus does not judge us but affirms us and accepts us as true members of the royal family. Schuller writes:

> Christ demonstrated such non-judgmental love that people flocked to Him, found and accepted forgiveness for their sins. He saw the potential for good in the worst of people. He wanted to bring out the best in them. How? By helping them to be redeemed from the guilt that kept reinforcing their negative self-image.[40]

In the previous chapter we noted that Schuller instructs his readers and viewers that they must give themselves to Jesus Christ to obtain the fruits of forgiveness. In typical evangelical fashion, he counsels people that they must be "saved" and "born again" before they can gain the positive self-esteem which will lead to peace, happiness, and success. Obviously he does not preface his "altar calls" with pleas for grinding repentence, but Schuller does seek to lead people toward decisions to accept Christ and his offer of forgiveness and new life. The following prayer, taken from

Self-Love: The Dynamic Force of Success, is a clear example of Schuller's evangelical call to commitment and a rather full expression of his doctrine of redemption:

> Jesus Christ, I accept You as my forgiving Savior. I don't understand what Your death on the cross means. But I know that in some way You died for me. I remember the old Jewish prophet who spoke about You when he said, "He was wounded for our transgressions, he was bruised with our iniquities, the chastisement of our sins was upon his shoulders." I remember an Indian chief who once said, "Fire cannot burn where fire has already burned." You have by Your suffering and death on the cross accepted the responsibility of my sins. You have fulfilled the justice that demands that wrong be punished. And you mercifully promise to extend this forgiving credit to my account. By Your death justice and mercy are both fulfilled. Thank You, Jesus Christ. Amen.[41]

Schuller holds to a rigorous doctrine of substitutionary atonement, but he gives it a new twist, relating it directly to self-esteem. Through his death on the cross, Christ experienced hell—total loss of self-esteem and eternal separation from God—thereby bearing our guilt and suffering for our sins. Forgiveness through Christ is so absolute that our sins are actually erased from God's memory. When we come to Christ in faith, God will treat us as "justified":

> "Just-as-if-I'd" never sinned
> "Just-as-if-I'd" never done anything wrong
> "Just-as-if-I'd" never felt guilty.[42]

This act of justification is unconditional. In no way did we earn or deserve the redemption from guilt and sin which Christ purchased from us upon the cross. It was an act of sheer grace.

Placing himself, on this issue at least, firmly in the tradition of Paul, Augustine, and Calvin, Schuller understands "justification by grace through faith" in forensic and judicial terms. God "declares" that we have been made righteous through Christ, and this declaration of grace is permanent. Yesterday, today, and tomorrow we have been set free from our burden of sin and guilt. To demonstrate the once-for-all nature of divine grace, Schuller likes to use the passage from Romans 4 where Paul writes that Abraham was declared righteous even before he was circumcised. Schuller glories in his own theological heritage: "My Calvinism gives me a base for self-esteem that I could not have if I were Arminian in my theology. Once I am truly redeemed I am declared to be righteous by faith."[43] Concerned that the foundation of grace be firm and absolute, Schuller rejects the ostensible Arminian, and perhaps Pelagian, position that it is possible to fall out of divine favor.

In Schuller's theological system, then, the process of redemption is ultimately directed toward restoring self-esteem. The act of atonement itself seems to be understood as a means to that end. In removing our guilt, Christ declares us to be righteous and thereby frees us to love ourselves. Schuller informs us that when Christ gives his followers "freedom from opprevise guilt," they come to know that they are children of God—"Suddenly their sense of self-dignity is restored." Christ is so important, not only because he forgives our sins and covers our guilt but also because he boosts our ego by accepting and affirming us. To make this point, Schuller tells us to imagine that someone even more important than the President of the United States, someone known as the Ideal One, invited us to his office to talk. How such an invitation would boost our self-esteem:

> When you meet this Ideal One, who knows you as you really are but treats you as if you were perfect, you have a psychological, existential, and spiritual encounter with the grace of God at the most profound level. That's when you are truly born again. Now you can also accept yourself.[44]

Christ stands at the very center of Schuller's redemptive process. As the Ideal One who died on the cross for our sin and guilt, Christ alone is able to declare us righteous and worthy of divine acceptance. This declaration of grace is "the ultimate capstone around which self-esteem is really wrapped." It is also the starting point for possibility thinking, for as we have learned in the preceeding chapter, it is impossible to achieve success in life unless we have a positive self-image. Christ's shameful death of crucifixion frees us to pursue our grandest dreams, or as Schuller puts it, "the cross sanctifies the ego trip."[45]

It should be added that the redemptive process whereby self-esteem is restored is not viewed as an end in itself, but as a means of equipping persons to Christ's work in the world. Christ honors us by "commissioning us to meaningful service." In the end, Schuller proposes a doctrine of self-esteem which "will bring glory to the human race for the greater glory of God."[45a]

Only in his recent writings has Schuller begun to elaborate what might be called "a theology of the cross." While he has always understood Christ's death on the cross as "central to our salvation," he has not wanted to identify this act as a symbol of defeat and despair. So Schuller has generally set forth a positive interpretation of the crucifixion. Christ's death upon the cross was not a personal defeat; it did not shatter his perfect self-esteem. Rather, it protected and purified the ego of our Lord, and it became a vehicle for unparalleled success.

Not that Schuller's positive theology of the cross negates the possibility of suffering, sacrifice, and self-denial. Attached to every dream is a price-tag:

> The higher the honor, the higher the cost. There is no crown without a cross. There is no success without sacrifice.

110

More and more, Schuller has come to emphasize that success involves service, involvement in the wants and needs of others. "Real success demands the sacrificial role, which by its nature calls for unselfishness and an attitude of sacrificial commitment."[46] But cross-bearing is ultimately a positive act, one which sanctifies our ego trips, builds our sense of self-worth, and leads to success in the world.

Schuller believes in the gospel of success, but he does not believe that success can be obtained without pain, conflict, and commitment. "Real success demands the sacrificial role, which by nature calls for unselfishness and an attitude of sacrificial commitment." Still, in line with his consistent emphasis upon human dignity, he wants to make a distinction between self-denial and self-debasement. He takes issue with those religionists who would equate self-denial with humiliation, who inspire persons "to think less of themselves than God thinks of them." Such attitudes are described by Schuller as "dangerous distortions and destructive misinterpretations of scattered Bible verses grossly misread by negative-thinking Bible-readers who project their own negative self-image onto pages of Holy Scripture."[46a]

Schuller has written little explicitly about sanctification, the other half of the great dyadic process of redemption, but I am convinced that in his lexicon we could substitute possibility thinking. Since we have discussed possibility thinking in the previous chapter, we will here simply connect it to Schuller's theological system. For Schuller, sanctification—or possibility thinking—is a post-justification process. Only after our self-esteem has been restored as a result of Christ's forgiveness and acceptance, are we able to pursue our goals in life through possibility thinking. At this point the process of salvation is pursued through self-help, as Christ has now freed us to become the persons we want to be.

It is clear that Schuller views possibility thinking as a vehicle for success, generally understood in terms of this-worldly health, happiness, and prosperity. Those disturbed by this consistent emphasis upon earthly concerns must be reminded that Schuller begins from the point of human needs; to make an impact on the essentially secular and materialistic person, Schuller stresses what will catch his or her fancy. It is also important to remember that the basic thrust of Schuller's appeal is similar to that of nearly all evangelical preachers: while they advertise eternal bliss, he advertises more immediate spiritual and emotional benefits. This is not to say that Schuller does not believe in the after-life. He is utterly orthodox on this point, but he does not stress it very much in his public ministry. Schuller is witnessing to an audience interested in immediate rather than long-range needs. They want a Christianity that bears fruits here and now.

Schuller has indicated that the theology of self-esteem has given rise to "additional, second generation theologies" which were born "like healthy children from healthy parents." Thus far, he has had time to do little more than introduce those five or six theological offspring.[47] But because they reveal a great deal about his ministry and the directions in which his thought seems to be going, I will state each of the corollary theological principles and give them summary treatment.

(1) *The Theology of Communication*: "I have no right to insult, embarrass or violate any person's dignity by written or spoken word."[48] Schuller has indicated that were he to write a book on communication, it would be developed around an aphorism discussed in an earlier section of this chapter. "I am not what I think I am; I am not what you think I am; I am what I think you think I am." Because people become what we expect them to be, it is crucial that we

are positive and supportive in our social intercourse. Schuller observes that there are many people who claim to be Christians, who read the Bible, and know all the right doctrines, but are "mean as the dickens" when it comes to communicating. We should never relate to people "by insulting, manipulating, or intimidating them."[49] If you can't say something positive about someone, say nothing.

(2) *A Theology of Evangelism*: "I have no right to offend the self-esteem of a person under the motivation or guise of 'saving his soul.' "[50] We have already discussed Schuller's strategy of evangelism, which is certainly an extension of his "theology of communication."

(3) *A Theology of Social Ethics*: "Any act or deed becomes unethical if it lowers—however immeasurably— that invisible but all-important mental climate in a community that I call a 'Society's Collectivized Level of Self-Esteem.' "[51] Schuller insists that all human beings are "blood relatives," part of "an organismic unity."[52] Therefore, any time a person does something—however personally satisfying—which is demeaning to himself or to others, then the members of the entire human family have been insulted and the collective level of self-esteem has been lowered. On this basis Schuller objects to suicide and abortion.[53]

(4) *A Theology of Economics*: An economic system must enhance the dignity of every individual in the economic community.[54] While Schuller has generally avoided discussing social issues, he has spoken out against Marxism and socialism, as well as capitalism, wherever those systems violate the freedom and self-worth of the individual. Contending that Marxism views man as "an intelligent computer made of bones, flesh and blood which functions best on sex and steak," Schuller predicts that it will ultimately fail for it "violates human dignity and militates against man's need to love himself."[55] Decrying any system which

is not based upon the autonomy of the individual, Schuller complains that state welfare tends to quash self-esteem. Insisting that poverty cannot be cured by handouts, Schuller suggests that the poor would gain much more if they were inspired by faith "to discover and develop their God-given abilities through Possibility Thinking."[56]

Schuller has warned that there are forms of capitalism which can stifle personal initiative and pride, but this economic system, based upon individualism and freedom, seems generally compatible with possibility thinking and a theology of self-esteem. In many respects his message actually serves as an inspirational apology for the American business community. It is not surprising, then, that he has been embraced by many of the country's most successful and wealthy Christian businessmen.[57]

(5) *The Theology of Government*: The ideal form of government is one that enhances individual freedom. Schuller glories in the democratic American system of government because it has, to his mind, guarded the freedom of the individual. Following the lead of certain historians, Schuller has suggested that American democracy was inspired by Calvinist theologians who held to the dignity of mankind as the cornerstone of faith.[58]

The purpose of this chapter has been to explain and analyze, rather than evaluate, the theology of self-esteem. An assessment of Schuller's message and ministry has been reserved for the final chapter of this book. Before moving into such an assessment, however, it will be helpful to see how Schuller's thought fits into the historical context of American religious culture. While there are many distinctive features to Schuller's approach, he does not stand alone with his message or his ministry. Many popular religionists before him have interpreted the Christian faith as a gospel of success.

The Gospel of Success in American Popular Religion

Robert Schuller is indirectly related to a long line of popular religionists who have proclaimed the gospel of this-worldly well-being through positive thinking. His lineage includes such disparate figures as Phineas Parkhurst Quimby, Mary Baker Eddy, Charles and Myrtle Fillmore, Ralph Waldo Trine, and Norman Vincent Peale. While there are many ideological branches on this family tree, all of its members have stressed a utilitarian message of self-help through some form of mind-conditioning. The roots which support it run deep into the fertile soil of American optimism, idealism, and individualism. To understand Schuller and his ministry it is necessary to become familiar with this side of his intellectual heritage. To be sure, Schuller has been more directly influenced by other religious traditions, most notably the form of Dutch Calvinism on which he was nurtured; but his pervasive message of possibility thinking reveals that among his spiritual ancestors are those who have developed and employed "popular psychologies aimed at health and wealth and peace of mind."[1]

The notion of success is deeply imbedded in the American ethos. Our national self-understanding has been significantly shaped by the popular belief that ours is an open and mobile society where individuals, uncircumscribed by class, sex, or race and strictly through their own efforts, are free to make whatever they will out of their lives. This collective conviction of unlimited opportunity has come to be known as "the American myth of success."[2] (Here the word "myth" does not imply something inherently false, but describes that complex of attitudes and values which shape our worldview and interpret our common experiences.) What is the meaning of success in America? As in all Western societies, success has been associated with wealth, power, and status, but because we have been so conditioned by the notions of autonomy and opportunity, we have tended to attach particular significance to the process of *achievement*. Those who earn rather than inherit position are generally most admired in our society. The greater the achievement, the more notable the success. Hence, the popularity of the "rags-to-riches" stories in which the road to wealth and power is long and paved with tortuous detours and dangerous potholes.

Because individual achievement has been the ultimate standard of success, it is not surprising that a self-help religious tradition has flourished in America. Eager to climb ladders of success, Americans have been attracted to those religious movements which have supplied self-help techniques and promised divine boosts to assist in the ascent. The earliest tradition of self-help identified success as a product of character and, therefore, stressed the virtues of industry, frugality, and prudence. This character strain of self-help emerged as a version of "the Protestant Ethic," which was spiritualized by the Puritans and then secularized by Benjamin Franklin. The self-made man (it was still a man's world) was he who conquered the world by living in accordance with a prescribed list of ethical maxims. In *The Way to Wealth*, Franklin listed two cardinal virtues, industry and frugality, and then added eleven more for good measure—temperance, silence, order, resolution, sincerity, justice, moderation, cleanliness, tranquility, chastity, and humility.[3] It was this understanding of success as a product of proper character development which pervaded popular culture during the nineteenth century. William Holmes McGuffey's famous "ecclectic readers" spread the message of success through diligence, assertiveness, and Christian charity to

116

more than one hundred million students during the century, and Horatio Alger did nearly as well with his hundred or so novels which seldom deviated from plots where success came to lost orphan boys who possessed plenty of pluck and luck.[4]

Most of those who promoted self-help through character formation warned against success's becoming an end in itself. Wealth, power, and position were to be gained for the glory of God and the good of one's neighbor. Success was generally considered as a means to an end. Even Russell Conwell, a strident success orator who delivered his "Acres of Diamonds" sermon more than 6,000 times during the early decades of this century (it was our "Christian and godly duty . . . to get rich") warned against making an idol out of money and urged responsible stewardship.[5] And while Conwell had raised the tone of the self-help message to a shrill pitch which would have disturbed the Puritans and even Ben Franklin, his emphasis was upon success as a product of certain character traits.

Conwell was the last of a dying breed of popular religionists. During the twentieth century, character-development would exercise only a minor influence upon self-help movements. Increasingly, those who advocated success through techniques of mind-cure have gained control of the self-help market. Schuller fits in this later tradition. While he certainly affirms the importance of character-development in his gospel of success, his message of possibility thinking is also built upon mind-conditioning and attitude-shaping. To be sure, his system is framed within the context of faith and prayer, but Schuller is convinced that the mind holds the key; he therefore belongs within the "mentalist" or "New Thought" tradition of self-help in America.

Those who have traced the lineage of New Thought have normally identified Phineas Quimby as its founding father. Quimby was a clock-maker from Belfast, Maine, who gave up this trade when he became involved in psychic healing during the 1830's. An itinerant mesmerist who used a hypnotic subject to make diagnoses of and prescriptions for diseases, Quimby soon determined that there was no causal connection between the prescriptions and the resultant cures. The medicine prescribed simply served as a placebo. Healing actually occurred because his patients *believed* that the medicine was effective. Quimby concluded, therefore, that disease was a mental problem and that health depended upon a mental cure. The New Thought or mind-cure movement took its departure from Quimby's proposition: "Disease being in its root a wrong belief, change the belief and it will cure the disease. By faith we are thus made whole."[6]

Believing this to be the single principle for all healing, Quimby abandoned mesmerism and hypnotism, and refined his process of mind-cure. He began to employ early forms of mental suggestion which would be further developed during this century by psychotherapists and by self-help religionists such as Schuller. While Quimby's initial approach was mundane and practical—based upon cause and effect—he gradually began to spiritualize his mental cure. From his mentalist starting point, he developed a form of theological idealism somewhat akin to Neoplatonism. He viewed man as a spiritual being who possesses an unconscious soul, which is directly related to and partakes in the divine mind. We are cured as we disabuse ourselves of wrong belief and touch base with our own divinity. Quimby became convinced that he had discovered the "science of healing" Jesus practiced when he performed his miracles.[7]

Though Quimby remained a relatively obscure figure throughout his lifetime, his spiritualized program of mental healing and mind-conditioning had a seminal influence upon nearly all those who represented the burgeoning New

Thought tradition during the latter part of the nineteenth century. Quimby's most famous protegee was Mary Baker Eddy, who so successfully popularized and institutionalized the theories of mind-cure. Cured by Quimby during the early 1860's, Eddy became, for a time, one of his most dedicated disciples and ardent supporters. While those who have claimed that Eddy plagiarized some of Quimby's unpublished manuscripts are probably mistaken, there can be little doubt that the mother of Christian Science owed a great intellectual debt to the father of New Thought.[8] Eddy's *Science and Health*, the virtual bible of Christian Science, clearly restates Quimby's "discovery" that disease is an error of the mind and that healing takes place through mental therapy. And if Eddy went even a step beyond Quimby in virtually denying the reality of the material world altogether, it was a logical conclusion to be drawn from Quimby's already intense idealism.

If Eddy was Quimby's most famous patient, it was Warren Felt Evans, a Methodist convert to Swedenborgianism, who became Quimby's actual successor. Successfully treated by Quimby for nervous exhaustion, Evans himself began to teach and write about Quimby's system of healing. During a twenty-year period, Evans produced a number of books, including *The Mental Cure*, *The Primitive Mind Cure*, and *Esoteric Christianity and Mental Therapeutics*, all of which reiterated the basic positions of New Thought.

Another important patient and disciple of Quimby was Julius H. Dresser, who in 1914 joined with two Christian Science exiles, Ursula Gestefeld and Emma Curtiss Hopkins, and a number of other mental healers to form the International New Thought Alliance. Unlike Christian Science, which was a tightly structured organization, the Alliance was a very loose confederation whose supporters "shared in the general hopes and tenets of mental healing spelled

119

out by Quimby and Evans.'' In 1916 the Alliance adopted a declaration of purpose which clarified the philosophical starting point of the movement. It read:

> To teach the infinitude of the Supreme one, the Divinity of Man and his infinite possibilities through the creative power of constructive thinking and obedience to the voice of the Indwelling Presence which is our Source of Inspiration, Power, Health and Prosperity.[9]

Two of the early supporters of the Alliance were Charles and Myrtle Fillmore, organizers of the Unity School of Christianity, which has been one of the most influential New Thought organizations. Healed through mind-cure techniques, the Fillmores became interested in making this form of "practical" Christianity available to people of all denominations. Thus, when it was organized in 1889, Unity was to be a "school" and not a church. To this day, direct competition with the churches has been avoided, but Unity has developed hundreds of "centers" where weekly services are held. Furthermore, an elaborate headquarters has been built outside of Kansas City to coordinate the activities of this thriving organization. The most distinctive feature of the school is a weekly prayer service, called Silent Unity, initiated by the Fillmores at the turn of this century. Today this prayer service is held round the clock at Kansas City, where hundreds of people handle the more than one-half-million annual requests for prayers. Charles Fillmore considered prayer to be the manner in which a person releases or activates the latent power of our mind:

> The spiritual ethers are vibrant with energies that, properly released, would give abundant life and health to all God's people. The one and only outlet for all these all-potential, electronic, life-imparting forces existing in the cells of our body, is our mind unified with the Christ mind in prayer.[10]

While prayer has been crucial to the development and popularity of the Unity School, the movement has promulgated its soft message of New Thought through various magazines, such as *Progress* and *Good Business*, as well as through television and radio advertising.

The early practitioners of New Thought, such as Quimby and Evans and Eddy, were essentially interested in mental healing, but their successors increasingly tapped the power of the mind as a souce of wealth as well as health. This shift of emphasis was subtle but significant. After all, if, as Quimby stated, disease was a problem of the mind, it followed that poverty was as well. Even in Eddy's system, which denied the reality of matter, there was a place for "supply" or economic success as proof of proper belief and divine favor. New Thought begins with the principle that God, as Spirit or Mind, is present everywhere and in everything. Since God is in all and through all, we must be a part of this Divine Mind, and our power must ultimately be mind power. What we are, then, is ultimately determined by our attitudes. If we think the proper thoughts, and use the divine power of our minds, we will be assured of health, wealth, and prosperity.[11]

Prentice Mulford was one of the successors of Quimby who grasped the full potential of mentalism as a means to this-worldly well-being. Already in the 1880's he began to proclaim to the world in bold print: "TO THINK SUCCESS BRINGS SUCCESS." Every thought, he informed his readers, was a power source as real as electricity. "Set the magnetic power of your mind persistently in the desire and *demand* of the best of everything; and the best will, by an inevitable and unerring law, eventually come to you."[12] Though he never became especially successful or well known himself, Mulford was a pioneer in the field of positive thinking.

While the New Thought movement of the nineteenth century attracted a fair percentage of those "come-outers" who have always lent vitality and diversity to American religion, it was generally regarded as sectarian and bizarre— or at best esoteric. Around the turn of the century, however, as the movement began to shift its emphasis from health to wealth, it gained an increasingly broad base of support among American Protestants. The first truly successful proponent of positive thinking as we know it today was Ralph Waldo Trine. Called by Yale historian Sydney Ahlstrom "the patriarch of the modern health and harmony tradition,"[13] Trine produced a genuine bestseller, *In Tune with the Infinite: Fullness of Peace, Power and Plenty,* in 1897. Over the years, this book sold an astonishing one and a half million copies. Trine's work contained all the basic precepts of New Thought. He wrote of the "soul life" which is connected to the Infinite Spirit through the "thought life." And, like Mulford, Trine understood this "thought life" to be "a vital, living force, the most vital, subtle, and irresistible force there is in the universe." Trine promises success to those who harness the power of positive thoughts. In a statement that would be echoed by Schuller, Trine advises those who face adversity to think about better things and more prosperous conditions:

> To hold yourself in this attitude of mind is to set into operation subtle, silent, and irresistible forces that sooner or later will actualize in material form what is to-day merely an idea. But ideas have occult power, and ideas when rightly planted and rightly tended, are the seeds that actualize material conditions.[14]

All of this, of course, is standard New Thought fare. Roy Anker, a student of self-help religion, tells us that Trine's popularity among traditional Protestants resulted from the fact that Trine, a skillful writer, "tended to blur some of the key differences between conservative Christianity and

New Thought." When choosing phrases, he "tended to use the language of tradition."[15] It is true that *In Tune with the Infinite* was a relatively benign statement of New Thought. But the popularity of the book surely had less to do with ideology than with inspiration. Trine's promise of prosperity for those whose thoughts were in tune with the Infinite inspired his many readers. Here was a book which not only sanctified success but supplied techniques guaranteed to help one achieve it.

With Trine's book a new form of religious literature was created that would become as common as aspirin by 1960. During the first half of this century, scores of writers and millions of readers would find themselves in tune with Trine. The stream of inspirational self-help literature was so heavy, says Ahlstrom, that "it is almost unwise to speak of individual writers; the books seem almost to have written themselves."[16]

Certain writers do, however, stand out. Two who belonged most solidly in the New Thought tradition were Emmet Fox and Glen Clark. Fox was a very popular minister in the Church of Divine Science whose "congregation" filled the Hippodrome and Carnegie Hall in New York. *The Power of Constructive Thinking* (1932) and *Make Your Life Worth While* (1942) elaborated techniques of mind-conditioning and proclaimed a message that "things are thoughts," and that external reality is "an outpicturing of our own minds."[17] Clark, who wrote a spate of inspirational books, including *The Soul's Sincere Desire* (1925) and *How to Find Health Through Prayer* (1940), was another confident proponent of mind-cure.

During the thirties and forties, a diluted form of New Thought began to find expression in the liberal tradition of American Protestantism. Grounded in a theological heritage which stressed God's immanence, human goodness, and cultural promise, the liberals were predisposed to certain underlying principles of New Thought. At any rate, some mainline Protestant writers produced very popular books which elaborated the themes of peace and power. E. Stanley Jones, a prominent Methodist missionary to India and a prolific inspirationalist, contributed such works as *Victorious Living* (1936), *Abundant Living* (1949), and *The Way to Power and Poise* (1949). And Harry Emerson Fosdick, the premier liberal who held the prestigious pulpit at Riverside Church in New York, produced a number of bestsellers which fit into the self-help genre of religious literature. His most important psychological interpretation of Christianity, *On Being a Real Person*, was published in 1943.[18]

Fosdick and Jones echoed the themes of New Thought in some of their writings, but Norman Vincent Peale was the mainline Protestant who truly popularized the message of success through positive thinking.[19] The son of a Methodist minister, Peale was a shy boy who overcame his deep feelings of inadequacy by perfecting his skills as a public speaker. When he graduated from Ohio Wesleyan in 1920, he intended to pursue a career in the newspaper business, but instead enrolled at the Boston University School of Theology after he realized that he could no longer resist his calling to the preaching ministry. A brilliant administrator and a superb communicator, Peale was immediately successful as a churchman. His Methodist congregations in Brooklyn and Syracuse grew rapidly—and so did his fame. And in 1932, at the age of thirty-five, Peale became the senior pastor at Marble Collegiate Church, a congregation on Fifth Avenue in New York City with a venerable Dutch Reformed heritage. For more than fifty years, then, Peale has held forth in that prestigious pulpit, bolstering the thousands who have constantly filled the pews with his time-tested brand of self-help Christianity. Beyond his direct influence at Marble Collegiate, Peale has inspired millions of Americans tuned in to national radio and television broadcasts of his sermons.

Peale has been one of the great pulpiteers of our age, but, ironically, he will probably be remembered more for his writings than for his preaching. While he began to issue a steady stream of inspirational books during the thirties, he made his first major impact upon the self-help book market when *A Guide to Confident Living* was published in 1948. On the bestseller lists for two years, it sold more than 600,000 copies and served as a prelude to Peale's most popular success book, *The Power of Positive Thinking*, which came out in 1952. This clearly utilitarian volume quickly sold more than two million hard cover copies, and stood for two years at or near the top of the bestseller lists. Reprinted repeatedly since the fifties, *The Power of Positive Thinking* has now sold millions of additional paperback copies, making it by far the most popular inspirational book of our time. While Peale has tried to work his literary magic again during the past three decades, none of his more recent books has matched the sales of these two early mind-power classics. It was during the cold-war era of the late forties and fifties when Americans were most attracted to Peale's positive and reassuring message. This does not mean, however, that Pealeism has lost its appeal. More than three and a half million people today subscribe to *Guideposts*, a magazine specializing in religious inspiration for successful living which has long been published and edited under Peale's auspices.[20]

Peale has admitted that he was directly influenced by New Thought during a crisis of relevancy early in his ministry.[21] While he does not explicitly promulgate New Thought ideology, there can be little doubt that he has incorporated much of its message and methodology into his relatively liberal framework of Christianity. *The Power of*

Positive Thinking, for instance, is a repository of the basic ideas and techniques that have characterized mind-power religion since the days of Ralph Waldo Trine. Following New Thought tradition, Peale's approach is pragmatic, based upon scientific principles that yield guaranteed results. In the introduction to *The Power of Positive Thinking,* Peale explains that the book "is simply a practical, direct-action, personal-improvement manual . . . written with the sole objective of helping the reader achieve a happy, satisfying and worthwhile life." Peale assures his readers that the principles set forth in the book were "firmly established as documented and demonstrable truth" by hundreds of persons who put them into practice. Here was no speculative or theoretical treatise. "This book teaches applied Christianity: a simple yet scientific system of practical techniques of successful living that works."[22]

Peale's scientific system is also based upon the principles of mind-conditioning. Echoing New Thought philosophy, Peale insisted that thoughts have power and that since we can control our thoughts, we have control of our own destinies:

> You can think your way to failure and unhappiness, but you can also think your way to success and happiness. The world in which you live is not primarily determined by outward conditions and circumstances, but by thoughts that habitually occupy your mind.

If we are what we think then the secret of success is to think success. Hence the power of positive thinking:

> This great law briefly and simply states that if you think in negative terms you will get negative results. If you think in positive terms you will get positive results. That is the simple fact which is at the basis of an astonishing law of prosperity and success. In three words: Believe and succeed.[23]

Like Trine, Peale identifies God as the immediate source of this mind-power which brings success. He views God as a Divine power plant which we must tap in order to obtain mental energy. "When in spiritual contact with God through our thought processes, the Divine energy flows through the personality, automatically renewing the original creative act." Peale insists that unless we are "in tune with the Infinite" we will never possess the necessary thought-power to obtain health, wealth, and personal happiness.[24]

Peale's self-help message quite clearly follows the basic constructs of New Thought. His writings do, however, signal a shift or emphasis in the mind-power tradition. While his mentalist predecessors harnessed the power of the mind to gain health and prosperity, Peale is more interested in personal wholeness, happiness, and peace of mind. Perhaps this is so because Peale has been a pastor to middle-class Americans who already had health and money but were still anxious, dissatisfied, and unfulfilled. Peale was a physician of the personality who offered a cure for this mental disease afflicting so many of his friends and parishioners. Positive thinking was really a form of psychological therapy linked to the religious principles of New Thought. The religio-psychiatric clinic established in 1937 by Peale and Dr. Smiley Blanton, a psychoanalyst, stands as a symbol of this fusion.[25] Religious healing and mental health had become one.

A remarkable octagenarian, Peale still preaches at Marble Collegiate Church, delivers speeches around the country, and writes articles and books which lay forth principles for successful living. But the Elijah of positive thinking has already found a successor. The mantle has fallen on Robert Schuller.

We have already taken note of the close relationship

between Schuller and Peale. Peale gave the up-and-coming young pastor a very good measure of identity and credibility, frequently speaking to the Garden Grove congregation and penning prefaces to some of Schuller's books. And there can be little doubt that Schuller has patterned the essential elements of his message after those of Peale. Schuller's possibility thinking closely resembles Peale's positive thinking, especially in terms of technique and methodology. Indeed, while the writing styles differ, Schuller's books are similar in approach to those of Peale—filled with aphorisms, anecdotes, personal testimonies, and "how-to" lists.

But Schuller is not simply Peale's clone. What makes Schuller interesting and noteworthy is the fact that he has linked principles of New Thought with American evangelicalism. Unlike Peale, who undergirded his positive thinking with liberal Protestant thought, Schuller has set his possibility thinking upon a more conservative theological foundation.[26] Not only do his books and television messages proclaim the need for conversion experiences and full-hearted commitments to Jesus Christ, but some of the most conspicuous and popular evangelicals have appeared as guest celebrities on "Hour of Power"—Corrie Ten Boom, Chuck Colson, and Joni Eareckson, among others. Furthermore, Schuller has been endorsed by such evangelical worthies as Billy Graham and W. A. Criswell, pastor of the powerful First Baptist Church in Dallas.

To be sure, Schuller seems an unconventional evangelical. Granted that "evangelical" is a slippery term today, eluding precise definition, Schuller must nonetheless be disconcerting to many who wish to claim such identity. His treatment of sin, for example, must bother certain evangelicals. And expository Bible preaching, another supposed pillar of evangelical Christianity, is hardly practiced by Schuller on his television program: "I admit I don't hold up a Bible. I don't deliver Biblical expositions. I don't jam the Bible down people's throats. I believe in the Bible, but if people want Bible preaching, they can get it elsewhere."[27]

There are other ways in which Schuller hardly represents stereotypical evangelicalism: he doesn't speak of damnation, Satan, the Second Coming, or separation from the world. But where I find him to be a particularly unorthodox—or at best, paradoxical—evangelical is in the message of possibility thinking itself. As we have seen, Schuller literally bids us to pull ourselves up by our own mental bootstraps. Certainly there is room for God in this process, as we are told to seek divine guidance and strength through prayer. And it is through Christ that we are freed to seek our grandest vision of success; or as Schuller puts it, "the cross sanctifies the ego trip."[28] But once we acknowledge God's grace and forgiveness, we must pursue success in altogether personal and mundane ways. Schuller's message is an interesting synthesis of evangelical grace and the New Thought principles of self-help. While he doubts that he has been directly influenced by the proponents of American New Thought, Schuller does not deny that he may have assimilated some of its mentalist methodologies. Convinced that no cult could be successful unless it had a truth to offer, he believes that such truths must ultimately be embraced and promulgated within the context of traditional Christian faith.[28a]

By several standards, then, Schuller is an unconventional evangelical. But while he may be unusual, he is by no means unique, for he is merely one of the most prominent of a large and growing group of evangelicals who are promulgating the gospel of success.

American evangelicalism has a long tradition of viewing religion as a vehicle to health, wealth, and happiness. Pentecostal revivalists like Aimee Simple McPherson, Kathryn Kuhlman, and Oral Roberts argued that physical healing is a blessing of the Spirit for those who have faith.

Others have emphasized material well-being. Revivalist A. A. Allen, for example, wrote a number of books on the theme of prosperity. These include: *The Secret to Scriptural Financial Success, Your Christian Dollar, The Power to Get Wealth,* and *God's Guarantee to Bless and Prosper You Financially.* Other evangelical books in this genre are *God's Master Key to Success and Prosperity,* by Gordon Lindsay; *God's Formula for Success and Prosperity,* edited by Oral Roberts and G. H. Montgomery; and *God's Will is Prosperity* by Gloria Copeland.

That many evangelicals have emphasized this-worldly success should not surprise us. Like other-worldly bliss, it is viewed as a gift of divine grace, one of the fruits of faith. Recently, however, some evangelicals have begun to advertise success through theories of self-help. In fact, it appears that the evangelicals are beginning to gain control of the religious motivation market, a market dominated in the past by eccentrics and liberals. Oral Roberts has typified this shift in evangelical thought. The faith healer of the fifties has developed a philosophy of success for the eighties which relies heavily on a positive mental attitude.[29] Other evangelicals should be mentioned as well. Zig Ziglar, a deacon at First Baptist, Dallas, has risen to the top with his top-selling motivational manual *See You At the Top,* while insurance entrepreneur W. Clement Stone produces *Success Unlimited* magazine, sponsors positive-thinking rallies, and advises us that with P.M.A. ("Positive Mental Attitude") "Whatever the mind can conceive and believe, it can achieve."[30] Along with Schuller's publications, evangelical books which echo the New Thought message include *The Miracle Motivation* by George Shinn, *The Pearl of Potentiality* by Dottie Walters, and *Reaching Your Possibilities Through Commitment* by Gerald W. Marshall. As Notre Dame historian Nathan Hatch puts it, "What seems to be in the works today is a convenient marriage of evangelical piety and self-help."[31]

In certain respects, then, the message of Robert Schuller may seem to be incompatible with the tenets of traditional evangelicalism. But if Schuller is an unconventional evangelical, he certainly does not stand alone. In this period of evangelicalism, many of the most prominent success evangelists represent the evangelical wing of Christianity. Mind-power, long a popular dimension of American religion, has now found a new evangelical formulation, but the basic message of health, prosperity, and happiness remains essentially unaltered by those who now insist that the old-time gospel has always been a gospel of success. Schuller's positive brand of evangelicalism seems indeed to have become a new orthodoxy.

CHAPTER VIII

Assessing Schuller's Message

It is ironic that Robert Schuller, who eschews controversy in the pulpit, has become so controversial a figure in the contemporary church. An exuberant, irrepressible, and confident spokesman for the gospel of success, Schuller seems to attract or repel. He has received both paeans of praise and criticism of the most cutting sort.

Schuller is supported not only by the millions who have been inspired by his "Hour of Power" telecasts and his possibility-thinking books, but also by thousands of clergy and church lay leaders who have benefited from his principles of church growth. But if success has brought support and imitation, it has also brought reproof, especially from some theologians and other members of the ecclesiastical establishment. As his popularity rose during the seventies, Schuller became the target of the sort of criticism which had been directed at Norman Vincent Peale during the late fifties. Some of the critics disapproved of Schuller's pulpit theatrics, others questioned the propriety of spending millions of dollars to erect an ecclesiastical edifice while millions of people throughout the world suffered in life-numbing poverty. The most devastating criticisms, however, were reserved for Schuller's positive message, which was interpreted as shallow and simplistic. As feared by one of his supporters, it appeared that "Schuller shooting" had become "a national sport."[1]

Schuller has not joined his critics in direct and public debates. Such a strategy of confrontation could only lead to negativism and thereby violate one of the cardinal principles of possibility thinking. Nonetheless, he has been stung and somewhat perplexed by the barrage of criticism which has been leveled at him. Most of his critics, he is certain, have misunderstood his ministry and misinterpreted his motives. Referring to some pastors who were complaining about the direction of his ministry in California, Schuller once replied, "They've made me cry more than once with their criticisms."[2] During the period when Schuller was constantly being questioned for building the Crystal Cathedral, he wrote that the price of leadership was high, but that in the end he would be vindicated. Plato was quoted to underscore the point: "I will live in such a way that I will prove by my life that my critics are liars."[3]

In the following assessment, I do not intend to join the muster of "Schuller-shooting" critics. I am convinced that too often Schuller's critics have taken cheap shots at him while failing to articulate and acknowledge the salutary features of his ministry and the genuine contributions he has made to the American church. On the other hand, while I wish to affirm many aspects of his ministry, I will pose what I believe are troubling questions about some of the ideological assumptions underlying his ministry. There are potential dangers along the path on which the gospel of success would lead the church.

FINDING THE GOOD AT GARDEN GROVE[4]

A few years ago, Schuller was asked to describe his role at Garden Grove. "I am," he suggested, "something like a show barker who cries out to the non-churched, 'Come in here, there's something good inside for you.' "[5] We must remember, then, that Schuller views himself as an apostle to the unchurched in America. He is above all an evangelist—or more accurately perhaps, a *pre*-evangelist who is primarily interested in attracting the attention of those who are indifferent to the organized church or wary of it. Driven by a desire to reach those who have written off the church as smug, archaic, and irrelevant, Schuller has developed a program which portrays the Christian faith as dynamic, accessible, and effective. The very symbols of Schuller's ministry reveal his central mission—open arms, an embracing smile, a spectacular building and ambience, entertaining worship services, and upbeat messages which promise success

So Schuller is essentially a "show barker" who invites the unchurched to come inside and listen to the gospel. Few religious leaders have performed that role with such consistency and effectiveness. While some of us may not be completely comfortable with the style and the substance of Schuller's ministry, we may certainly admire its scope and approve its strategy.

Schuller is a nationally recognized religious leader, but his most impressive ministry perhaps has taken place at the local level. The congregation in Garden Grove has served as a laboratory where the principles of church growth could be tested and marketed. The "Garden Grove Experiment" was conducted on the premise that prospective members should come from the ranks of the unchurched in Orange County. From the beginning, therefore, the worship services and various ministries of the congregation were geared primarily to meet the needs of unchurched. In fact, as the church has grown, Schuller has continued to insist that the needs and concerns of the nonmember be placed one notch higher than those already members. Today there are more than 10,000 persons claiming membership in the congregation which began so inauspiciously at the Orange Drive-In a little more than twenty-five years ago. The Garden Grove Experiment has been a singular success. But still concerned about those driving by the church on the surrounding freeways, and still convinced that the church must serve first as a "mission station," Schuller continues to set his sights on membership growth.[6]

The Crystal Cathedral is a publicity agent's delight. What could be easier than to promote a congregation which boasts 10,000 members, a spectacular glass and steel worship center, one of the world's largest pipe organs,[7] and a dynamic silver-haired senior pastor who appears on television each week? But those who visit the church, lured perhaps by all the symbols of success, soon discover that behind the mind-boggling statistics, glass buildings, and possibility preaching is a congregation genuinely engaged in ministry. In addition to those programs in which the members themselves participate—a lay ministry training center, a counseling clinic, a literacy center, a day-care program, and other specialized ministries—major mission projects are supported indirectly through congregational funding.[8]

To be sure, much credit for the Garden Grove programs must go to the unsung members of the staff and the laity who bring Schuller's grand visions into daily operation; but Schuller has unquestionably orchestrated the tone and the tempo of the ministry. Those who come in contact with the congregation are almost always impressed not only by the forms of ministry taking place but also by the fact that such a large congregation can demonstrate such warmth and openness.

Having tested his principles of church growth at the Garden Grove laboratory, Schuller decided to share the secrets of his success through the Robert H. Schuller Institute for Successful Church Leadership. The Institutes have been well received by church leaders for three reasons. First, he inspires a change in attitude about ministry itself. Schuller's enthusiasm is contagious, and most participants return to their churches with renewed vision, hope, and energy. Second, Schuller provides practical principles. One mainline minister noted that the Institutes were so worthwhile because Schuller "delivered direct, clear, common-sense material of inestimable help to any pastor or lay leader who can . . . learn the principles underneath and translate them into his or her own situation."[9] And third, in a more general sense, Schuller demonstrates that growth will occur only when the church is turned inside out, when there is a deliberate effort to attract the unchurched. What Schuller shares is a perception of the church which identifies mission as its primary function.

Participants in the growth institutes do not necessarily become Schullerites. But one should not underestimate the impact Schuller's growth strategy is having upon the contemporary church in America. All across the country, churches have begun to change the style and direction of their ministry, hoping to catch the attention of those on the outside looking in. Overall, such changes are beneficial.

Best known and most highly visible of the Schuller ministries, of course, is the "Hour of Power." In this popular production various facets of the man and his mission coalesce. We need not approve every facet of "Hour of Power" to appreciate its general thrust. Like most television ministries, this program relies on promotional techniques, the "give-to-get" money solicitation ploy, simplified, repetitious messages, and the star syndrome. But notwithstanding the criticism one may have of these techniques, the "Hour of Power" seems to be functioning effectively as a ministry of pre-evangelism. While it is essentially a telecast of one of the worship services at Garden Grove, the production is hardly parochial or sectarian. It may emanate from within a church, but it is beamed at the non-churchgoer as well as the churchgoer. The music is not churchy, the guests are often celebrities, the prayers are inclusive, and the messages are invariably positive. The already committed are inspired and bolstered by this celebration of positive Christianity, and the uncommitted are invited to come inside and discover more about the Christian faith. While it is evident that the majority of the viewers of the "Hour of Power" are already church members, it is also true that Schuller seems to attract a larger percentage of non-Christians and nominal Christians than most of the other primetime preachers.[10] His constructive, nonthreatening, and nonjudgmental approach is not only consistent with his message of possibility thinking; it is the centerpiece in his strategy to gain a hearing from the unchurched. Fully aware that his viewers are free to flip channels, he has designed his service to be as attractive, entertaining, and inoffensive as possible. The "Hour of Power" has been rated by Nielsen and Arbitron as the top weekly religious broadcast.[11] Apparently, Schuller's strategy is working.

I have not intended here to offer a blanket endorsement of Schuller's ministry, but to credit him with developing a bold and comprehensive mission to the unchurched in America. Ultimately, his most significant contribution will be in this area of ministry. "Schuller's gift to the contemporary church," as one participant in a growth institute expressed it, "is largely in his genius for winning a hearing from the unchurched. Regardless of our theology or our politics or our location, we can learn from him."[12]

ASSESSING SCHULLER'S MESSAGE

A fair assessment of Schuller's thought must begin with the acknowledgment that it has taken shape within the context of an ongoing mission to the unchurched. In the introduction to *Self-Esteem: The New Reformation* Schuller reveals that his "human-needs" approach reflects the fact that his ministry has been "a mission to the unbelievers" for more than thirty years.[13] Interested in a message which would undergird a successful mission strategy, Schuller has developed the theology of self-esteem, so attractive because it stresses healing and wholeness without threatening judgment and triggering guilt. Nearly every dimension of this theological system seems to reinforce this positive mission perspective. While certain that his theological enterprise is a faithful contemporary expression of the traditional Reformed thought he learned at Hope College and Western Theological Seminary, Schuller acknowledges that the theology of self-esteem—at base, a theology of mission—is the North Star of his entire system.[14] The following sections, then, raise questions, not about the basic mission approach, but about some of the directions which this approach seems to take.

The Gospel and Success

Schuller proclaims a gospel of success, and he does it unabashedly. Few popular religionists, even those standing in the New Thought tradition, have so enthusiastically identified the Christian faith with the success ethic. Certain that God wants us to be winners, Schuller encourages us to believe in ourselves, to be bold about our goals, to dream impossible dreams. "Believe in success," he urges, "for success means discovering God's beautiful plan for your life and allowing it to develop to its fullest potential."[15] Possibility thinking, the trademark of Schuller's ministry, is above all a self-help formula for success. As proof that the formula is potent, Schuller points to his own career. But more interestingly, he also refers to the life of Christ. Christ is the greatest possibility thinker who ever lived because he used the cross as a strategy to attract followers who ultimately built one of the largest organizations in the history of humankind—the universal church. Christ, says Schuller, "is the super success of all times . . . I am not following a loser, I am following a winner."[16]

Since Schuller has been accused of developing a doctrine of success which is crassly materialistic, we must review what he means by success. He seems to operate with two definitions. In his general definition he stresses accomplishment or achievement. A successful person is one who attains a self-defined goal. In this context success may or may not mean health, wealth, happiness, peace of mind. When Schuller tells us to turn mountains into goldmines, he is encouraging us to accomplish a great goal; he is not baptizing the pursuit of riches.

Schuller has provided a narrower definition of success to answer those critics who might complain that his doctrine of success, if not necessarily materialistic, is at least self-serving. "Success," Schuller now tells us, "is building self-esteem in yourself and others through sacrificial service to God and your fellow human beings!" From a Christian point of view, this definition certainly makes Schuller's success system more attractive. Success is connected to service and is not directly linked to this-worldly gain, but to self-esteem. Schuller expands on the latter point: "You may accumulate riches, fame, and honors, but unless you achieve tremendous self-esteem in the process, all that the world calls success becomes ashes in your hands."[17] We must notice, however, that Schuller's second definition still measures success by a standard of self-service, the achievement of self-esteem. So in the end, Schuller has given us a doctrine of success which converges nicely with his "human-needs" mission approach. While the system is not necessarily materialistic, it nonetheless centers on the self.

Is Schuller's understanding of success compatible with the Christian faith? It is undeniable that certain sections of the Bible hold forth a success ethic. The Deuteronomic literature is grounded upon the conviction that God blesses his chosen people when they are faithful and obedient, and removes his blessings when they are not. Many of the great prophets base their messages upon the same mechanical view of reward and punishment. This theme also reverberates through portions of the Psalms: "The Lord knows the way of the righteous, but the way of the wicked will perish" (Psalm 1:6). In many respects, Proverbs can be read as a success manual, one of the first religious how-to books. Throughout the Old Testament, the success ethic is radically theocentric. Success was always a result of obedience and contingent upon service. However, this black-and-white view of reality was seriously undermined by the writers of Ecclesiastes and Job. In Job, the "orthodox" view was explicitly challenged as a good and faithful man endured failure, pain, and sorrow, seemingly without cause.

The New Testament expands upon the apparently divergent themes raised in the Old Testament. On the one hand, the New Israelites, the followers of Christ, will be blessed with strength, comfort, and peace: "Come to me, all who labor and are heavy laden, and I will give you rest" (Matthew 11:28); "Peace I leave with you; my peace I give unto you. . . . Let not your hearts be troubled; neither let them be afraid" (John 14:27). Moreover, those who do the work of the kingdom are to expect their efforts to be blessed, for the kingdom is like a grain of mustard which will grow into a mighty tree, or like leaven which works mightily throughout the meal (Matthew 13). The book of Acts is certainly a great success story: the gospel reaches thousands throughout the Mediterranean world, spreading through concentric circles from Jerusalem to Rome. So the refrains of blessing and success echo through the New Testament as well.

On the other hand, the New Testament also picks up the theme introduced by the writer of Job. If Christians are to know success it will not necessarily be understood in this-worldly terms. They were warned to count the cost of discipleship because the way of the Lord could mean rejection, suffering, and death: "Whoever does not bear his own cross and come after me cannot be my disciple" (Luke 14:27). The Christian is called to obedience and service, but the rewards are not to be measured in terms of fame, wealth, or physical comfort. The orthodox success ethic seems to have been turned on its end. The righteous did not receive prosperity; they were persecuted. John the Baptist was decapitated by Herod Antipas. Paul, who suffered a thorn in the flesh throughout his ministry, was repeatedly imprisoned before being shipped off to Rome. Peter, it is believed, was crucified upside down in Rome.

A Christian must interpret success in terms of obedience to God and service to those in our midst. Yes, Jesus was a superlatively successful person—not, however, because he founded a great organization, but because he bent his will to the heavenly Father, and as a suffering servant—despised, rejected, and forsaken—experienced the ignominy of death upon the cross. This is the Christ who is our success model.

Schuller's success orientation is attractive because it identifies success with those achievements which build esteem in self and others through sacrificial service. Though he believes that the traditional interpretation of "bearing our cross" has been unduly oppressive and negative and therefore needs to be reformed along more positive lines, Schuller insists that "there will be no success without self-denial and cross-bearing."[18] The cross of commitment, then, serves to sanctify our grandest dreams of success on the grounds that others will be served and God will be glorified as we bolster our self-esteem.

The problem with Schuller's success gospel arises from the fact that success seems to be a means to self-esteem rather than a byproduct of obedience to God. A Christian should not be ultimately concerned with failure or success but with doing the will of God. Obedience to God may well bring us higher self-esteem, but that is not the issue. In gaining higher self-esteem through achievement we may indeed serve others and bring glory to God, but that is not the issue either. Obedience to God and service to those around us should be our primary concerns, our chief ends—that is what it means to be a Christ-like success. Jesus has reminded us that members of his kingdom need not be anxious about their lives because God knows our needs: "But seek first his kingdom and his righteousness, and all these things shall be yours as well" (Matthew 6:33).

In his ministry Schuller has learned that a positive success-oriented message catches the attention of the unchurched in America. While he has carefully stated in recent writings that success is tied to service and sacrifice, there is always the danger that those who are attracted to his possibility-thinking message may mistakenly identify it as a means to personal gain, most often wealth, power, and status. The means by which Schuller attracts people to the church creates the impression of material success—a 10,000 member congregation, a magnificent glass and steel worship center, a million-dollar budget, one of the world's largest pipe organs, and so on. The "scars-to-stars" stories told by Schuller and his weekly guests often reinforce this image of success. Those who stay to scratch beneath the surface of the gospel learn from Schuller that success carries the price tag of commitment, but the body language of his ministry says something quite different. All of this demonstrates how difficult it is to balance means and ends when proclaiming the Christian faith. A pre-evangelist, Schuller has developed a message of success which risks being misunderstood by some, with the hope that it will lead others toward a meaningful faith. Apparently it is a risk he is willing to take.

143

The Christian and Self-Esteem

During the mid-seventies, students of American culture began to document a growing interest in self-fulfillment, especially among the younger generation. Tom Wolfe wrote about the "Me Decade," while Peter Martin described the self movement as "the New Narcissism." Christopher Lasch in *The Culture of Narcissism* brilliantly expanded upon the thesis that in this age of diminishing expectations, Americans were becoming increasingly self-ist in their search for meaning, pleasure, and fulfillment.[19] While there are indications of a more recent shift away from this self-obsession, it is probably true that we are still indulging in the new narcissism.

The gospel of self has been most effectively promulgated by the many pop psychologies which have been so evident on the paperback racks—bestsellers like *Games People Play*, *I'm O.K.—You're O.K.*, *Your Erroneous Zones*, and *Looking Out for #1*. These books have tended to be popularized versions of self-theories which have been propounded by humanistic psychologists such as Erich Fromm, Rollo May, Abraham Maslow, and Carl Rogers. Despite the diversity of their approaches, these theorists share an interest in human freedom and potential for self-actualization.

The religious book market reveals that Christians as well have become deeply involved in the self-movement. Observes John Stott, "a whole new literature" has sprouted in support of Christian self-affirmation.[20] Numerous evangelical writers have been imploring us to love ourselves almost as a moral and theological duty. Certain that you are out of practice, Cecil Osborne demonstrates the *Art of Learning to Love Yourself*; Walter Trobisch tells you simply to *Love Yourself*; and Bryan Jay Cannon insists that you must *Celebrate Yourself*. Schuller certainly belongs in the ranks of these self-help Christians.

The theology of self-esteem has made three significant contributions to the contemporary church. First, Schuller has helped to make us aware of the pivotal role self-esteem plays in our lives. Many psychological studies point to a direct relationship between self-esteem and personal well-being. Individuals with weak self-images are less likely to be happy, healthy, poised, fulfilled, mature, and successful than are those with strong self-images.[21] On the basis of such findings, psychologists like Nathaniel Branden have concluded that a person's self-evaluation is "the single most significant key to his behavior."[22]

Second, the theology of self-esteem serves as a healthy antidote to the theology of self-negation which still persists in certain strains of American evangelicalism. It is generally agreed that evangelical pulpiteers have too often reinforced negative self-images with relentless messages of sin, guilt, and depravity. Buttressed by hymns which have urged Christians to loathe and abhor themselves, these sermons have effectively communicated a message of human worthlessness. Certain that far too many preachers have shared the sentiments of the clergyman who stated, "I feel I've preached an effective sermon when I've left my congregation feeling guilty," Anthony Hoekema warns that unless balanced by the biblical message of forgiveness and affirmation "such preaching may indeed create in the hearers a negative self-image which may take years to erase."[23]

And third, Schuller has correctly identified the gospel as the ultimate resource for building self-esteem. Despite the Fall, God has neither abandoned his wayward children nor counted them as worthless. Indeed, God so valued us that he sent his Son to suffer and die on a cross that we might be redeemed and renewed. Schuller is certainly right when he argues that God's acceptance of us in Christ is "the ultimate capstone around which self-esteem is really wrapped."[24] Because God loves us we are able to love ourselves. Hoekema effectively argues that Christians have often failed to realize the promise that they are new beings in Christ (II Corinthians 5:17), free authentically to love God, neighbor, and self. "We have been writing our continuing sinfulness in capital letters, and our newness in Christ in small letters," writes Hoekema. "When the Christian faith is accepted in its totality, that faith brings with it a predominantly positive self-image."[25]

Schuller's theology of self-esteem supplies us with necessary corrections, then, to theological systems which stress self-negation and self-abasement, but with its stress upon the self, his system may lead to a dangerous form of Christian narcissism. Having identified inadequate self-esteem as the essential human problem, Schuller interprets the gospel as the ultimate remedy for this condition. It is through Christ, his death and resurrection, that we have not only been set free from our sins, but also set free from crippling low self-esteem. Pronounced worthy by God through Christ, we are able to accept and affirm ourselves and begin to appropriate God's grandest dreams for our lives. The cross becomes the foundation upon which to build a program of self-help through possibility thinking.

This system, however, so appealing as a starting point for mission theology, focuses too intently upon the self. Schuller does not mean this to happen, for he does wish to place the theology of self-esteem within a theocentric context. Reflecting his Reformed heritage, he has written that a faith rooted in self-esteem "will bring glory to the human race for the greater glory of God."[26] But as one concerned about "human needs," Schuller has concentrated upon theology as it relates to self-esteem. Such a focus upon the self may lead to a sort of narcissism or self-love, which Schuller himself warns against.

According to Reinhold Niebuhr, Augustine helps us to identify such narcissism when he makes a biblical distinction between two forms of self-love—"that in which the self loves itself simply and that in which the self loves itself in God."[27] When we are truly new beings *in Christ*, then our lives take on a wholly new perspective; the self has an object beyond itself. Paul expresses this radical concept when he writes to the Galatians, "I have been crucified with Christ: it is no longer I who live, but Christ who lives in me; and the life I now live in the flesh I live by faith in the Son of God, who loved me and gave himself for me" (2:20). Proper self-love is that which is not self-directed but centered in and through and for Christ who is in us.

The Christian faith is more than a vehicle for self-fulfillment and self-actualization; it is also a call to self-giving and self-forgetting. Much of the narcissism circulating through the church today is inappropriate given these words of Jesus: "If any man would come after me, let him deny himself and take up his cross and follow me. For whoever would save his life will lose it, and whoever loses his life for my sake will find it" (Matthew 16:24-25). It is the paradox of the gospel that when our lives become Christ-centered, given over to service and sacrifice, we begin to discover the meaning of proper self-love. Christ himself is the supreme model for this sacrificial love:

> His state was divine
> yet he did not cling
> to his equality with God
> but emptied himself
> to assume the condition of a slave
> and became as we are;
> and being as we are,
> he was humbler yet
> even accepting death,
> death on a cross (Philippians 2:6-8)[28]

Karl Barth once observed that the greatest freedom we can experience is freedom from the self.[29] Isn't that the gospel promise? Not that we have been freed by Christ to love ourselves but that we have been set free from self-obsession. Not that the cross frees us *for* the ego trip, but that the cross frees us *from* the ego trip. In removing our sin of self-centeredness, in enabling us to forget the self, Christ has freed us to focus upon God and those around us. Christ negates our narcissism.

Sin and Self-Esteem

In assessing Schuller's doctrine of sin, we must begin by recalling that he makes a critical distinction between the "first sin" and original sin. It is his position that the sin of Adam and Eve was that of willful rebellion, but that the consequence of this "first sin" is that their children have been "born in the jungle" detached from a truly trusting relationship with the heavenly Father. The original sin, then, the sin which has afflicted humankind through the ages, is really lack of trust, a weakened self-esteem rather than willful pride. To be sure, Schuller recognizes that we are affected by destructive pride, but he understands this to be one of the negative fruits of the Fall—a "defense mechanism" triggered by an insecure ego.[30]

By thus identifying original sin as weakness rather than willful pride, Schuller lays the groundwork for a positive evangelistic approach. Unlike Adam and Eve, who chose to disobey God, their children need to hear a message of affirmation and acceptance. Furthermore, this doctrine of the Fall carefully protects the fragile shell of dignity which all humans share as children of the Father. Schuller is not Pelagian at this point, for he belives that apart from Christ, the children of the Fall are wholly incapable of gaining the requisite self-esteem. Retrieving a phrase he learned at seminary, Schuller speaks of "total inability" rather than "total depravity,"[31] a term so often employed by Calvinists. Salvation, or the restoration of sufficient self-esteem, is therefore utterly impossible apart from the grace of affirmation which is offered through Jesus Christ. Schuller's understanding of original sin is consistent with his overall theological system, but it also evokes some crucial questions. What is the true relationship between sin and self-esteem? Is the essence of our sinful condition that of willful pride or inadequate self-esteem? Is our sin rooted in fact in weakness or in rebellion?

These questions have exercised theologians for centuries. While the Augustinian strain, which identifies pride as the essential sin, has dominated the Western traditions, especially those which stem from the Protestant Reformation, other traditions have understood it to be lack of trust or lack of faith. Those standing in the Augustinian tradition will argue that the original sin which we share with all human beings, including our spiritual parents, is a tendency to glorify or deify ourselves. It is this vibrant pride which has caused us again and again to rebel against God. It is because we have loved ourselves too much, not too little, that we have, as Paul wrote, "exchanged the glory of the immortal God for images resembling mortal man" (Romans 1:23).

Schuller has given us a doctrine of sin upon which he builds a consistent theology of self-esteem. But did not Augustine correctly read the human heart when he insisted that self-deification was the essential sin? "What is pride but undue exaltation? And this is undue exaltation, when the soul abandons Him to whom it ought to cleave as its end and becomes a kind of end in itself."[32] Calvin seems to understand this well when he writes that there is "nothing that man's nature seeks more eagerly than to be flattered," adding that "blind self-love is innate in all mortals."[33]

In our fallen condition, do we truly lack confidence and self-esteem? Some important recent psychological studies argue otherwise; they reveal pervasive "self-serving" or "self-justifying" tendencies. People readily accept credit for their successes and good behavior, but reject blame for their failures and bad behavior. According to these studies, most people rate themselves well above average in socially acceptable traits (for example, considerateness, ethics, ability to get along with others). They more readily accept as true flattering descriptions of themselves than unflattering descriptions. They justify as right whatever acts they have committed. Summarizing dozens of research studies pointing to these self-serving biases, one research psychologist was moved to paraphrase Elizabeth Barrett Browning: "How do I love me? Let me count the ways."[34] Such studies, of course, are provisional, but they hint at biases that are basic to our human condition and not merely a disguise for an essential weakness.

While Schuller admits that he avoids actually mentioning "sin," he disagrees with those who claim that he fails to deal with sin in his ministry. Believing that sin manifests itself wherever personal and social problems appear, Schuller argues that he attacks sin constantly, but through offering positive solutions rather than negative judgments. "I deal with sin all the time at a place where it erupts in human pain, not at a place where it erupts in human shame."[35]

It does seem unfair to say that Schuller fails to deal with sin. Moreover, he is probably correct when he chides negative-thinking theologians for looking at the doctrine of repentance "through distorted glasses tinted with a mortification mentality." Granted, too few people realize that repentance (*metanoia*) is, as Schuller writes, "a positive creative force . . . a turning of one's life from sin to the Lordship of Christ."[36] But if we need to emphasize more strenuously the fact that repentance means new life in Christ, we must not fail to stress at the same time the necessity of coming to terms with our old life. Paul writes that we must put off the old nature before we put on the new (Ephesians 4:22-24). In the same vein, Calvin wrote that we must undergo a radical self-examination, for such knowledge "will strip us of all confidence in our ability, deprive us of all occasion for boasting, and lead us to submission."[37] And it was Wesley who claimed that we must confront Christ as sinners "inwardly and outwardly destroyed."[38] Reminding us that the majestic Reformation doctrine of grace follows a doctrine of depravity, historian Nathan Hatch reiterates another paradox of the gospel: "that it must crush self-righteousness before uplifting the contrite; that it must root out self-centeredness before offering consolation; that it must kill off self-will before unveiling the power to live by."[39] A gospel that does not point to the depth of human misery and deceit cannot bring us to the height of grace.

Psychology and the Gospel

Schuller was once asked what profession he would have chosen if he had not become a minister. "An existential psychologist," he replied. "I think that's what I am now—a psychologist who is a theologian."[40]

It is apparent from his messages and books that Schuller has been influenced by a variety of psychological methodologies, including cognitive therapy, psycho-cybernetics, and psycho-therapy, as well as existential or humanistic psychology, which is most often associated with Erich Fromm, Abraham Maslow, Rollo May, and Carl Rogers. Open to many approaches, Schuller has been no slave to any single tradition, but in a general way his thought most reflects an existential approach. It must be noted here that this influence has been indirect, for Schuller insists that he has not read the works of some of the prominent existential theorists.[41] Nevertheless, many of the basic principles of his possibility thinking bear a striking resemblance to the following summary of existential therapy:

> Existential therapy starts with the isolated self, aware of its basic existence but confronted by non-existence and the associated emotion of dread. This self, valued and accepted directly by the therapist, is encouraged, in the

face of non-being, courageously to commit its self to self-defined decisions that will bring its potential to fulfillment. This transcendent activity, or becoming-through-choosing, also creates the essence of the individual. On the other hand, failure to fulfill self-potential causes guilt. When this process succeeds, an individual who initially had only an existence has now created his own essence.[42]

Schuller is to be applauded for recognizing the inherent value of the psychological approach, and beyond that for urging cooperation between psychologists and theologians. Certain that an unhealthy tension has too long existed between the two disciplines, he suggests that supposed contradictions in thought can be "reconciled on the altar of truth." What is needed today, he says, "is a theological restructuring which synergizes scientific and spiritual truth as related to the human being."[43] Efforts at cooperation of this sort must be encouraged, but it is to be wondered whether biblical truth and psychological truth are, as Schuller suggests, one and the same.[44] There may be some good reasons to question whether existential psychology and the Christian faith are comfortable bedfellows.

In his tough-minded book *Psychology as Religion: The Cult of Self-Worship*, Paul Vitz has pointed out that the foundations of American ego-psychology are inherently "selfist." The self is absolute and autonomous, the determiner of its own existence completely unhindered by outside pressures or forces. Carl Rogers put it explicitly: "I am the one who chooses. . . . I am the one who determines the value of an experience for me." Vitz, a psychologist himself, is deeply disturbed by this "literal self-deification," and by what he considers to be existential psychology's uncritical assessment of human nature. He suggests that Maslow, for instance, regards humanity "as essentially good and never evil." Vitz concludes that a psychological tradition which obscures or denies so many biblical principles can hardly supply a foundation for Christian therapy.[45]

It would be inaccurate to say that Schuller has built his theological system solely upon the foundation of existential psychology. We have noted the pivotal role which Christ plays in Schuller's therapy—a factor which sets him apart from the secular psychologists. But if the theology of self-esteem moves beyond existential therapy, it is nevertheless undeniably a psychologized version of the gospel. At the very least, Schuller has converted biblical concepts into psychological concepts. That in itself raises a crucial concern. Nathan Hatch asserts that the recent union of evangelicalism and the self-help movement has been based upon the assumption that it makes little difference if we replace the biblical concepts of moral poverty, selfish blindness, and spiritual nakedness with the more fashionable psychological notions of fear, frustration, and anxiety.[46] One might claim, like Schuller, that this is merely a matter of putting traditional ideas into modern idioms. But something important is often lost in the translation. When the biblical notion of willful human pride becomes the psychological equivalent of a defense mechanism to cover insecurity, there is legitimate cause for concern. While psychology can tell us a great deal about the human condition, it does not study humanity in relation to God. Psychology is inherently anthropocentric. Christianity focuses upon human concerns, but from a perspective which is rigorously theocentric.

Positive Thinking and the Christian Faith

With his possibility thinking, Schuller has perpetuated "the American mystique of the mind."[47] Convinced that the mind is the control center of reality, he has developed a process which helps us to condition our minds with positive thoughts, which in turn lead to positive actions. While Schuller is obviously a physician of the spirit who prescribes prayer and a relationship with Christ for a healthy self-esteem, he is also a physician of the mind who prescribes positive thinking as a sort of panacea for life's problems.

153

We must acknowledge what secular inspirationalists and motivators have always known—that positive thinking is an effective technique for self-improvement. Hundreds of psychological studies indicate that those who believe that they have control over their destinies are more likely to be independent, obtain higher marks in school, make more money, and attain more long-range goals than those who do not believe in themselves.[47a]

Positive thinking seems also to affect our bodies. Much is already known about the effect of attitudes and emotions on physical well-being. Hospitals and doctors' offices are filled with patients whose ills are psychosomatic. The practice of psychosomatic and holistic medicine is already part of our health programs. Mind and matter have been acknowledged as partners in the quest for physical health. The nineteenth-century practitioners of mind-cure apparently were on to something. Recent research supports Schuller's claim that there is a connection between positive attitudes and chemical changes in the brain cells. Bio-psychologists have long known that the brain secretes certain chemicals into the blood stream which affect the way a body functions. Panic and fear, for instance, tend to increase catecholamines in the blood, which affect the heartbeat. Today we are learning that many attitudes—despair, depression, determination, confidence—help or inhibit the secretion of various body chemicals—endorphins, enkephalines, epinephrine, gamma globulin, and interferon, among others. While it will take much more research to prove definitively the physiological basis for positive thinking, it seems likely that such evidence will be found.[48]

Up to a point, then, possibility thinking works. When we block out our negative emotions, ''imagineer'' our dreams, meditate upon inspiring verses, repeat positive mantras, and visualize our goals, we are likely to move closer to our version of success—whether it be happiness, health, or peace of mind. I do not question the efficacy of positive thinking, nor do I wish to dissuade Christians from employing it as a technique for self-improvement. I do, however, suggest that there are two potential weaknesses in this approach.

First, positive thinking is an inadequate perspective from which to view life. Reality is not merely mind-deep, as some positive thinkers would have us believe. All of us are buffeted about by external pressures and forces over which we have no control. As body-beings, we have been created with certain physiological incapacities which cannot be transcended through mind power. This is true of our mental capacities as well. While it is true that few of us come close to realizing our full mental capacity, there are physiological limits to our native intelligence. When Schuller enthuses, "Whatever the Mind Can Believe the Human Being Can Achieve,"[49] he means to inspire us to live up to our God-given potential; but such inspirational statements may also be misleading. As Christians we accept the limitations of creaturehood. We affirm our mortality. It is in our finiteness, in the realization that we are ultimately incapable of shaping our own destinies, that God comes to us in grace.

The second problem with the positive approach is that it encourages us to evade the negative aspects of life. This does not mean, at least in Schuller's system, that we deny the negative aspects of life, but in accord with his therapeutic approach, that the negative should not be allowed to stifle positive creative thoughts and actions. We are to exorcise negative thoughts from our minds, for like unwanted weeds they crowd out positive thoughts and thereby block success. We should not even utter the negative ten-letter word "impossible."[50]

It is certainly true, as Schuller suggests, that many preachers have been "negatively prophetic" in their ministries, creating unnecessary conflicts and polarizations without offering meaningful solutions. There is a place for a ministry like Schuller's, which he describes as ''positively prophetic,'' in that it attacks personal and social ills with a constructive message of self-esteem.[51] Still, the positive-thinking approach can move us too quickly and facilely from an honest confrontation with the harsh realities of misery and meaninglessness in our world. The Bible offers little support for the notion that the negatives can be avoided. There we find a balanced picture of life, with its unvarnished woes as well as its golden possibilities. Jeremiah anguished for the people of Judah who were about to be exiled by the Babylonians; Job complained to God from an abyss of despair; Jesus lamented that his Father had forsaken him in death. In a world desperately needing strong biblical remedies, the positive perspective must always be informed by a radically realistic analysis of the human condition.

Culture and the Christian Agenda

Schuller's church-growth strategy is founded upon the principles that non-Christians should set the agenda for the church. ''Discover the *cultural tempo* of the unchurched people,'' Schuller tells the participants at his Institutes. ''Go out and make a big, inspiring impression on those non-churched people! And they'll come in!''[52]

But there are inherent dangers in allowing the culture to set the agenda for the church, for the history of the church has too often told of cultural captivity. Christians in the past have been all too ready to embrace the values and standards of their host culture, thereby often muting the prophetic call to justice, love, and humility before God.

Robert Schuller has become an international religious figure, and his principles of self-esteem have been hammered out in dialogue with Christian leaders from other cultures.[53] Still, his embrace of the American way has at times become quite explicit. Periodically, he has held patriotic worship services for his congregation and the viewers of "Hour of Power." The services have included rousing patriotic hymns and anthems and often a rendition of "I Am the American Flag," a first-person soliloquy which Schuller first preached during the Viet Nam era, when dissidents were questioning American values. In an introduction to the published version of the message, Schuller revealed why it had first been preached. "Always, in our nation," he wrote, "there are negative thinkers who deluge us with cynical, gloomy, pessimistic predictions that would discredit our country. At an hour like this I suggest listening to the American flag."[54] At a recent patriotic service in the Crystal Cathedral, which included a band from the Armed Forces, Schuller repeated the now-famous sermon while the congregation viewed a huge flag which had been attached to the girders of the sanctuary.[55]

Schuller does not often whip up patriotism in the manner of some of the God-and-country stars of the electronic church, but such demonstrations do reinforce the religious nationalism which is so deeply rooted in the ethos of American Christianity. It can become a cultural idol which ought to be exposed rather than worshipped. A land of freedom and opportunity, America rightly engenders our respect and loyalty. But the church must be very careful not to yoke the gospel to any form of civil religion, for it transcends all national entities. Nationalism is a powerful cultural religion which far too often has domesticated the church.

Schuller tends to identify the Christian way with the American way in other respects as well. As we have noted, one of the corollaries to the theology of self-esteem is a theology of economics which seems to serve as a religious philosophy for certain forms of capitalism. Early in his ministry, Schuller explicitly blessed the gospel of private wealth:

> You have a God-ordained right to be wealthy. You are a steward of the goods, the gold, the gifts, that God has allowed to come into your hands. Having riches is no sin.

> Wealth is no crime. Christ did not praise poverty. The profit motive is not necessarily unchristian![56]

Such a statement is certainly dated. The Schuller of today would not want his ministry to be identified with an expression which appears so materialistic and self-serving. Yet he would still support an economic system which is based upon the profit motive. In his recent writings, Schuller has linked his self-esteem system to a Theology of Economics which inspires "a noble incentive impulse in the human spirit."[57] He seeks to propose a philosophy centered in human dignity which can transcend the tensions between socialist Christians and capitalist Christians, but the cornerstone of his system seems to presuppose some form of private enterprise. It is little wonder, then, that his ministry has been consistently supported by Christian members in the American business community.

It is not my intention to criticize Schuller's economic philosophy but to question whether it should be so directly linked to the Christian faith. There is, of course, evidence from the book of Acts that members of the early church shared their money and goods.[58] However one wants to exegete such biblical passages, the gospel does not seem to offer direct support for a profit-oriented economic system. Actually the New Testament seems not to endorse any particular social or economic system for the general population. It does hold to a Christian way of life which is God-centered and other-directed.

Faithful to his own strategy of church growth, Schuller has allowed the culture to set the agenda for his ministry. There are times, however, when Christians must step back from their milieu and pose sharp challenges to cultural norms and values. The church is always in a tenuous position vis-à-vis culture—it is to be *in* but not *of* the world. It must translate the gospel into cultural terms without becoming acculturated.

Robert Schuller has been one of the most prominent and influential leaders of the American church during the last half of the twentieth century. He has been a successful pre-evangelist who has learned to bring the unchurched within earshot of the gospel. Bold, imaginative, inspiring, he has been a major force in the continuing church-growth movement, sharing secrets of his success at Garden Grove with thousands of church leaders who have benefited from his principles. Only the most cynical observers could deny that he has brought comfort and hope to millions suffering from distress and despair through his popular television ministry.

Like most popular religionists, Schuller has come under attack for promulgating a message which lacks depth and variety. Some of this criticism is unjustified, for he has recently begun to elaborate a theology of self-esteem to provide the ideological foundation for his ministry. Notwithstanding such efforts, however, Schuller remains something of a "johnny-one-noter"[59] who seldom varies his positive approach to the gospel. Essentially, he has been an "apologist" for the Christian faith who has consistently shaped the gospel message so that it might gain a hearing from those who stand outside the church—hence, Schuller's concern to ameliorate the tensions which have existed between theology and psychology, the church and culture, the sacred and secular. Convinced that these "schizophrenic splits" hinder Christian missions, he has sought "to synchronize the sacred and the secular."[60] This certainly seems to be a laudable goal, for our Christ *is* the Christ of culture. At the same time, however, we must realize that Christ stands *above* culture. In the end we must acknowledge that there are tensions, perhaps paradoxes, inherent to the gospel which will always resist resolution. The melodies of the faith which Schuller plays for us are invariably positive, culture-affirming refrains. But in the full orchestration of the faith there are not only soaring melodies but arresting counter-melodies as well. When all the parts are there, the gospel is a wonderful symphony of salvation.

ENDNOTES

Chapter I
"Scars into Stars: The Making of a Possibility Thinker"

1. Sheila Schuller Coleman, *Robert Schuller, My Father & My Friend* (Milwaukee: Ideals, 1980), pp. 34-35.

2. While no truly satisfying single-volume histories of the Reformed Church in America have been published, several surveys are available. See Arie R. Brouwer, *Reformed Church Roots* (New York: Reformed Church Press, 1977); Dennis E. Shoemaker, *A People of Hope* (New York: Reformed Church Press, 1978); Howard E. Hageman, *Lily Among the Thorns* (New York: Half Moon Press, 1975); and Elton M. Eenigenburg, *A Brief History of the Reformed Church in America* (Grand Rapids: Douma Publications, 1958). Other helpful treatments of the Reformed Church in America include Gerald F. De Jong, *The Dutch Reformed Church in the American Colonies* (Grand Rapids: Wm. B. Eerdmans, 1978), Edward T. Corwin, *A Manual of the Reformed Church, 1628-1902* (New York: Board of Education of the Reformed Church in America, 1902); and James W. Van Hoeven, ed., *Piety and Patriotism* (Grand Rapids: Wm. B. Eerdmans, 1976).

3. Coleman, *op. cit.,* p. 24.

4. *Ibid.,* pp. 19-20.

5. Robert H. Schuller, *Move Ahead with Possibility Thinking* (Old Tappan, N.J.: Spire Books, 1967), p. 18. For another version of this story, see Coleman, *op. cit.,* p. 20.

6. *Move Ahead,* p. 18. In an interview with Beth Amante ("Saving his Flock from Garbage," *The Grand Rapids Press,* Sun., April 19, 1978, Wonderland section, pp. 2-4), Schuller said that the seeds of possibility thinking took root "as an infant" and that the concept developed as he "studied psychology" (p. 2).

7. Coleman, *op. cit.,* p. 22.

8. Included in Robert H. Schuller, *The 10 Best Messages* (Garden Grove: Hour of Power, 1980), p. 53

9. Schuller relates a number of these Depression recollections in Jan Roorda, "A Call to Live Joyously," *The Saturday Evening Post* 250 (April 1978): 57.

10. *Ibid.* See also *Move Ahead,* pp. 175-78.

11. Coleman, *op. cit.,* p. 22.

12. Schuller has periodically plugged his alma mater on the "Hour of Power." In an interview with the author (June 4, 1980, at Garden Grove), he indicated that his "compulsion to excellence" was shaped by his Hope College education.

13. Coleman, *op. cit.*, p. 38. Schuller remembers being captivated by California. "I was so impressed with the beaches, surf, and trees, it was like another world." Quoted in Cynthia Marsh, "Positive Thought Helped in a Tragedy," *The Grand Rapids Press*, April 9, 1979, p. 5B. The other members of the Arcadian Four were Warren M. Hietbrink, Kenneth Leestma, and William J. Miedema. Like Schuller, all three served Reformed Churches in California.

14. Amante, *op. cit.*, p. 2.

15. Robert H. Schuller, *Your Church Has Real Possibilities!* (Glendale, Calif.: Regal Books, 1974), p. 59. Schuller's mentors at Western Seminary are reluctant to criticize him, but they would probably question the claim that he is an authority on Calvin. See Joel Clark, "Packaging Jesus," *The Grand Rapids Press*, Sun., April 9, 1978, Wonderland section, p. 4.

16. Coleman, *op. cit.*, p. 34.

17. Arvella plays an increasingly important role in her husband's ministry. She sits in on important staff meetings, assists in the direction of the "Hour of Power" telecasts, and spearheads certain on-going programs at Garden Grove. When I asked the staff at the church about those who truly had Schuller's ear on critical matters, I was told that members of his family, particularly his wife, were his most trusted advisors.

18. *Move Ahead*, p. 18.

19. Robert H. Schuller, *Peace of Mind Through Possibility Thinking* (New York: Jove/HBJ Books, 1978), pp. 172-73.

20. Coleman, *op. cit.*, p. 41.

21. *Your Church*, p. 10. See also *Move Ahead*, pp. 18-19.

Chapter II
"The Garden Grove Experiment"

1. See C. Peter Wagner, Foreword in Robert H. Schuller, *Your Church Has Real Possibilities* (Glendale, Calif.: Regal Books, 1974), no pagination.

2. Schuller, *Move Ahead with Possibility Thinking* (Old Tappan, N.J.: Spire Books, 1967), p. 19.

3. *Ibid.*, p. 20. Schuller mentions the matter of mimeographed bulletins in *Your Church*, p. 159. Apparently the printed (rather than mimeographed) bulletins were used only for special occasions during the early years at Garden Grove, for daughter Sheila remembers helping her mother and father run off bulletins on a primitive mimeograph machine. See Sheila Schuller Coleman, *Robert Schuller, My Father & My Friend* (Milwaukee: Ideals, 1980), p. 63.

4. *Your Church*, p. 160.

5. *Ibid.* The same story is told with a slightly different twist in *Move Ahead*, p. 21.

6. Coleman, *op. cit.*, pp. 43-44. Schuller's was not the first drive-in ministry. In fact, while on their honeymoon in June 1950, Robert and Arvella had attended a Lutheran drive-in service at Spirit Lake, Iowa.

Schuller mentioned this while lecturing at the Institute for Successful Church Leadership.

7. *Your Church,* pp. 160-61.
8. *Move Ahead,* pp. 22-23, and *Your Church,* pp. 112-14.
9. *Move Ahead,* pp. 24-25.
10. *Your Church,* pp. 114-16.
11. *Ibid.,* pp. 162-64. For more on the Rosie Gray story, see *Move Ahead,* pp. 26-27.
12. *Move Ahead,* pp. 28-29.
13. *Ibid.,* p. 30.
14. *Ibid.,* pp. 30-32, and *Your Church,* pp. 166-69.
15. *Move Ahead,* pp. 32-33, and *Your Church,* p. 165.
16. *Move Ahead,* p. 34.
17. Schuller, *Peace of Mind Through Possibility Thinking* (New York: Jove/HBJ Books, 1977), pp. 11-12. The first church building, on Chapman Avenue, had been designed by a young Long Beach architect, Richard Shelley. Some members had insisted that it was unnecessary to secure an expensive independent architect. On his own initiative, Schuller secured Shelley, who designed a beautiful structure. Going first-class paid dividends later for the building was sold for a $40,000 profit in just three years. Schuller remembers that it was "the most beautiful church building" in the area. "Good architecture," Schuller surmises, "is always a good investment." In line with that principle, when the drive-in walk-in church was planned, the congregation secured Neutra, according to Schuller, "the foremost living architect in the world at that time" (*Your Church,* pp. 165, 169).
18. The stone tiles in front of the sanctuary have been set in a rather unusual vertical (rather than horizontal) arrangement. A tour guide explained that the architect deliberately used this pattern to underscore the positive, heavenward thrust of the ministry. See also *Your Church,* p. 124.
19. *Move Ahead,* pp. 35-36.
20. *Time* and *Newsweek,* barometers of popular American religion, have favored Schuller and his ministry with frequent coverage over the years. See "Drive-In Devotion," *Time* 90 (Nov. 3, 1967): 83-84; "Spiritual Shopping Center," *Newsweek* 78 (July 5, 1971): 51-52; "Retailing Optimism," *Time* 105 (Feb. 24, 1975): 38-39; "Park and Pray," *Newsweek* 87 (May 10, 1976): 103, 106; "People," *Time* 115 (May 26, 1980): 87; "The Crystal Cathedral," *Newsweek* 96 (Oct. 6, 1980): 97; "Joyful Christmas Sounds and Sites" (a picture and paragraph describing the Christmas service at the Crystal Cathedral), *Time* 116 (Dec. 29, 1980): 6-7.
21. *Your Church,* p. 173.
22. *Ibid.,* pp. 173-74. For the dedication of the Tower of Hope see Ann Terrill, "Grove Church Renders Dramatic Service," *Orange County Register,* Sun., Feb. 22, 1970, Leisuretime section, pp. 2, 3, 10; and Anne La Riviere, "Dial 'New Hope' for Counseling," *Los Angeles Times,* March 21, 1969, Sec. IV, pp. 1, 8.
22a. Schuller, in an interview with the author at Garden Grove, March 3, 1983.
23. Calvin Tompkins, "Profiles: Forms Under Light," *The New Yorker* 53 (May 23, 1977): 43.

24. *Ibid.*, p. 44.

25. John Dreyfuss, "Star-Shaped Crystal Cathedral to Soar 12 Stories," *Los Angeles Times*, Sept. 26, 1976, pp. 1, 10; and Steve Emmons, "All-Glass Church: A Pane to City," *Los Angeles Times*, Jan. 15, 1977, pp. 1, 10.

26. Tompkins, *op. cit.*, p. 44. See also Robert Lindsey, "Opening of Glass Cathedral is Feast for Eyes and Ears," *The New York Times*, May 15, 1980, p. A20.

27. See Schuller, *The Peak to Peek Principle* (Garden City, N.Y.: Doubleday and Co., 1980), pp. 162-71.

28. *Ibid.* See also Ronald Yates, "From Outdoor Theater to 'Cathedral'—a Religious Success Story," *The Chicago Tribune Magazine*, July 27, 1980, pp. 10-11, 23-24, 26. Also Schuller, in an interview with the author at Garden Grove, March 3, 1983.

29. Yates, *op. cit.*, pp. 10-11.

30. Martin Bernheimer, "Crystal Cathedral Opening," *Los Angeles Times*, May 15, 1980, Sec. IV, pp. 1, 3; Yates, *op. cit.*; and John Dart, "Minister's Vision in Glass Built with Mottoes and Millions," *Los Angeles Times*, Sat., Sept. 13, 1980, Sec. I-A, p. 1.

31. Wendell Karsen, "The Crystal Cathedral Distorts 'Success,' " *The Church Herald* 38 (Jan. 23, 1981): 17. In following issues the letters to the editor reflected sharply divided attitudes about the Crystal Cathedral. See "Letters," *The Church Herald* 38 (Feb. 20, 1981): 19; (March 6, 1981): 21; (March 20, 1981): 18-19; and (April 3, 1981): 19.

32. See Yates, *op. cit.*, p. 23; and Schuller, "How to Make Your Dreams Come True," in *The 10 Best Messages* (Garden Grove: Hour of Power, 1980), p. 73.

33. Emmons, *op. cit.*, p. 12. The "money-generating factory" statement was released by the church and may not have been directly quoted from Schuller. The release also mentioned that the building would contain "4100 income-producing seats"; see also Eileen Beyer, "Robert Schuller: Crystal Persuasion," *News from Hope College* 12 (Oct. 1980): 8-9; and John Dreyfuss "Opulent Setting of the Crystal Cathedral," *Los Angeles Times*, Sept. 18, 1980, pp. 1, 22, 23.

34. "The Crystal Cathedral," *Newsweek* 96 (Oct. 6, 1980): 97. Yates, *op. cit.*, p. 10.

35. For some recent discussions of this age-old debate see Ronald J. Sider, "Cautions Against Ecclesiastical Elegance," *Christianity Today* 23 (Aug. 17, 1979): 15-19; and Thomas Trumbull Howard, "Expensive Churches: Extravagance for God's Sake?" *Christianity Today* 23 (Aug. 17, 1979): 19-23.

36. "Crystal Cathedral: Dedication Sunday, September 14, 1980" (brochure distributed at the dedication services). See also Elaine Beno, "Cathedral to Open in Services Sunday," *Orange County Register*, Sept. 13, 1980, pp. A-3, A-11.

37. Beno, "Cathedral," pp. A-3, A-11, and "The Crystal Cathedral," *Newsweek* 96 (Oct. 6, 1980): 97. Cousins' comment is reported in the *Cathedral Chronicle* 5 (Sept. 1981): 1.

38. Paul Goldberger, "Architecture: Johnson's Church," *The New York Times*, Tues., Sept. 6, 1980, p. C7.

Chapter III
"Sharing the Secrets of Success"

1. C. Peter Wagner, Foreword in Schuller, *Your Church Has Real Possibilities* (Glendale, Calif.: Regal books, 1974), no pagination. A spate of church growth books has been published to date, including Donald McGavran, *Bridges of God: A Study in the Strategy of Missions* (New York: Friendship Press, 1955); *How Churches Grow: The New Frontiers of Mission* (London: World Dominion Press, 1959); *Understanding Church Growth* (Grand Rapids: Wm. B. Eerdmans, 1970); C. Peter Wagner, *Your Spiritual Gifts Can Help Your Church Grow* (Glendale, Calif.: G/L Publications, 1979); *Our Kind of People: The Ethical Dimensions of Church Growth in America* (Atlanta: John Knox, 1979).

2. McGavran's endorsement was included in an advertisement for the tenth anniversary of the Institutes held at Garden Grove, October 22-26, 1980. I found one of the ads in *Christianity Today* 24 (June 27, 1980): 775. Wagner's endorsement is found in the Foreword to *Your Church*, cited above.

3. Schuller, *Your Church*, Preface, no pagination.

4. *Your Church*, p. 30.

5. *Ibid.*, pp. 59-60. Schuller credits Dr. John Piet of Western Theological Seminary with pointing out that traditional Calvinistic doctrines of the church do not possess adequate doctrines of missions. In an interview with the author at Garden Grove, March 3, 1983.

6. Wilfred Bockelman, "The Pros and Cons of Robert Schuller," *The Christian Century* 92 (Aug. 20-27, 1975): 732-35; and Schuller, *Your Church*, pp. 25-27.

7. See Philip Nobile, "Robert Schuller: Possibility Preacher," an interview in *The Long Island Press*, Sun., Feb. 3, 1974, p. 38.

8. Quoted in Bockelman, *op. cit.*, p. 733; see also *Your Church*, pp. 48-58.

9. *Your Church*, p. 58.

10. *Ibid.*, pp. 45-46.

11. *Ibid.*, pp. 117, 128.

12. *Ibid.*, pp. 45, 135-140.

13. *Ibid.*, pp. 62-66.

14. *Ibid.*, pp. 66-67.

15. *Ibid.*, pp. 67-68.

16. *Ibid.*, pp. 17-19; see "Spiritual Shopping Center," *Newsweek* 78 (July 5, 1971): 51-52; and "Retailing Optimism," *Time* 105 (Feb. 24, 1975): 38-39.

17. *Your Church*, pp. 19-29.

18. *Ibid.*, pp. 1-2.

Chapter IV
"The Hour of Power"

1. Jeffrey K. Hadden and Charles E. Swann, *Prime Time Preachers: The Rising Power of Televangelism* (Reading, Mass.: Addison-Wesley, 1981), p. 30.

2. *Ibid.*, pp. 73-74. See also Ben Armstrong, *The Electric Church* (Nashville: Thomas Nelson, 1979), pp. 19-52; and J. Harold Ellens, *Models of Religious Broadcasting* (Grand Rapids: Wm. B. Eerdmans, 1974), pp. 38-68.

3. Hadden and Swann, *op. cit.*, pp. 81-83.

4. For surveys of the principal television ministries today, see *ibid.*, pp. 17-45; Armstrong, *op. cit.*, pp. 100-21; and Charles E. Swann, "The Electronic Church," *A.D.* 8 (Oct. 1979): 17-20.

5. Armstrong, *op. cit.*, p. 10.

6. For a discussion of the debate over the number of Americans who actually tune in to the religious telecasts, see Hadden and Swann, *op. cit.*, pp. 47-67; and William Martin, "The Birth of a Media Myth," *The Atlantic* 247 (June 1981): 7, 10, 11, 16. Recent studies indicate that the television ministers tend to exaggerate the number of people who regularly view their programs. Even the top rated "Hour of Power" and "Oral Roberts and You" attract little more than two percent of the households in a ratings coverage area (Martin, p. 11).

7. Reported by Ron Kirkpatrick, "Pastor Parlays Drive-In Sermon into National Fame," *Orange County Register*, March 5, 1978, pp. A1, A3, A4, A10; and Schuller, *Your Church Has Real Possibilities* (Glendale, Calif.: Regal Books, 1974), p. 93.

8. *Your Church*, pp. 94-95. Arvella Schuller tells parts of the same story in an interview with the editor in *Creator* 2 (Jan. 1980): 12-13.

9. *Your Church*, p. 95; and Arvella Schuller interview, and Mike Nason, "Televising Your Worship Service," *Creator* 2 (Jan. 1980): 33.

10. *Your Church*, pp. 95-96.

11. Arvella Schuller, *op. cit.*, p. 14.

12. Quoted in Kirkpatrick, *op. cit.*, p. A4.

13. Nason, *op. cit.*, p. 34; and Nason, interview with the author at Garden Grove, June 4, 1980.

14. The Neilson figures were reported with pride in the *Cathedral Chronicle* 5 (Sept. 1981): 1-2; the Arbitron figures are reported in *The Church Herald* 40 (March 4, 1983): 22.

15. The Arbitron study (Feb. 1980) is cited in Hadden and Swann, *op. cit.*, pp. 51-62.

16. Schuller, in an interview with the author at Garden Grove, March 3, 1983.

17. Quoted in Hadden and Swann, *op. cit.*, p. 117.

18. Quoted in Phyllis Mather Rice, "Robert Schuller: Man with a Mission," *Your Church* 24 (Sept./Oct. 1978): 16.

19. *Ibid.*; see also Arvella Schuller, *op. cit.*, p. 18.

20. Arvella Schuller, *op. cit.*, p. 16.

21. *Ibid.*, pp. 16-17.

22. *Ibid.*, pp. 16-18.

23. Schuller, interview with the editors of *The Wittenburg Door* 25 (June-July 1975): 11.

24. *Ibid.*, p. 13.

25. See *Your Church*, pp. 129-39; and "Schuller Answers Critics," *Orange County Register*, March 5, 1978, p. A3.

26. Quoted in George Vecsey, "Preacher Who Pioneered Drive-In

Religion Gains Followers With His Upbeat TV Show," *The New York Times,* Tues., Oct. 11, 1977, p. 25.

27. For a good general analysis of these issues see Jeffrey K. Hadden, "Soul-Saving via Video," *The Christian Century* 97 (May 28, 1980): 609-13.

28. For example, Hadden and Swann call Schuller "The only mainliner on the marquee of religious broadcasting" (*op. cit.,* p. 29).

28a. A recent American Research Bureau study, "Profile of the Christian Marketplace," indicates that television ministries seem to empty neither the pews nor the coffers of the local churches. Reported in "TV Evangelism: Billy Graham Sees Danger Ahead," *TV Guide* 31 (March 5, 1983): 8.

29. Quoted in Ronald Yates, "From Outdoor Theater to 'Cathedral'—a Religious Success Story," *The Chicago Tribune Magazine,* July 27, 1980, p. 10.

30. Quoted in William F. Fore, "There is No Such Thing as a TV pastor," *TV Guide* 28 (July 19, 1980): 16; and in Armstrong, *op. cit.,* p. 10.

31. Hadden has bemoaned the lack of empirical evidence on this issue. See his "Soul-saving Via Video," p. 612. For a positive assessment of the electronic church's impact upon the local congregations, see Armstrong, *op. cit.,* p. 151.

32. See Yates, *op. cit.,* p. 26.

33. John Mariani, "Television Evangelism: Milking the Flock," *Saturday Review* 6 (Feb. 3, 1979): 25.

34. See Hadden and Swann, *op. cit.,* pp. 100-102.

Chapter V
"Possibility Thinking"

1. Three other Schuller books bear the ubiquitous possibility-thinking label: *It's Possible!, Your Church Has Real Possibilities,* and *Positive Prayers for Power-Filled Living.*

2. Schuller, *Reach Out for New Life* (New York: Bantam Books, 1977), p. 1; and Schuller, *You Can Become the Person You Want to Be* (Old Tappan, N.J.: Spire Books, 1973), p. 12.

3. Schuller, *The Peak to Peek Principle* (Garden City, N.Y.: Doubleday and Co., 1980), p. ix; and *You Can Become,* p. 12.

4. Peale, for example, wrote the Introductions for *Move Ahead with Possibility Thinking* and *Self-Love: The Dynamic Force of Success. You Can Become the Person You Want to Be* was dedicated to Peale.

5. Schuller, *Peace of Mind Through Possibility Thinking* (New York: Jove/HBJ Books, 1978).

6. *Reach Out,* p. 3.

7. *Ibid.,* pp. 24, 28.

8. *You Can Become,* p. 61.

9. *Peak to Peek,* p. ix.

10. See Phyllis Mather Rice's interview with Schuller, "Robert Schuller: Man with a Mission," *Your Church* 24 (Sept./Oct. 1978): 8.

11. Schuller, *The Greatest Possibility Thinker That Ever Lived* (Old Tappan, N.J.: Fleming H. Revell, 1973), pp. 1-12, 22. See also Philip Nobile, "Rev. Robert Schuller: Possibility Preacher," *The Long Island Press*, Sun., Feb. 3, 1974, p. 38.

12. See Rice, *op. cit.*, p. 8.

13. *Peak to Peek*, p. 29.

14. *Reach Out*, p. 10; and *Peak to Peek*, pp. 28, 34.

15. Schuller "Turn Your Scars Into Stars," in *The Ten Best Messages* (Garden Grove: Hour of Power, 1980), p. 65.

16. Schuller, *Turning Your Stress into Strength* (New York: Fawcett Gold Medal, 1978), p. 12.

17. *Reach Out*, p. 29.

18. *You Can Become*, pp. 15-16, 91. In *Move Ahead with Possibility Thinking* (Old Tappan, N.J.: Spire Books, 1967), Schuller writes of the "Disadvantage Complex" which hinders so many from achieving success (pp. 39-44).

19. *Reach Out*, p. 24; and Schuller, *Self-Love: The Dynamic Force of Success* (Old Tappan, N.J.: Spire Books, 1969), p. 84.

20. Schuller, *Discover Your Possibilities* (New York: Ballantine Books, 1978), p. 112.

21. *Ibid.*, p. 152.

22. *You Can Become*, pp. 39, 122.

23. *Ibid.*, pp. 39-46.

24. *Move Ahead*, pp. 14-15, 39-54.

25. *Ibid.*, pp. 56-57, 60-63.

26. *Ibid.*, p. 62.

27. *Peace of Mind*, pp. 130-37.

28. *Reach Out*, p. 177. A similar list is found in *You Can Become*, pp. 130-39.

29. Printed in this form in *You Can Become*, p. 37.

30. *Move Ahead*, p. 50-51.

31. *Ibid.*, p. 46.

32. *Ibid.*, pp. 158, 167-68.

33. *Ibid.*, pp. 178-80; and *You Can Become*, p. 131.

34. *Reach Out*, pp. 162-67.

35. See *Peak to Peek*, pp. 10-13. See also Robert and Arvella Schuller, *The Courage of Carol* (Irvine, Calif.: Harvest House, 1978).

36. *You Can Become*, pp. 12, 65.

37. Some articles that point in this direction are Norman Cousins, "The Mysterious Placebo: How Mind Helps Medicine Work," *Saturday Review* 4 (Oct. 1, 1977): 8-12, 14, 15; Leslie L. Iversen, "The Chemistry of the Brain," *Scientific American* 241 (Sept. 1979): 134-49; Mark R. Rosenzweig, Edward L. Bennett, and Martin C. Diamond, "Brain Changes in Response to Experience," in *The Nature and Nurture of Behavior*, ed. W. T. Greenbough (San Francisco: W.H. Freeman and Co., 1972), pp. 117-24; and Norman L. Mitchell, "You Are What You Think," *Ministry* 55 (May 1982): 26-27, 29.

38. See Schuller's interview with the editors of *The Wittenburg Door* 25 (June-July 1975): 11.

39. Chapter title in *You Can Become*, p. 140.

40. *Discover*, p. 112.
41. John M. Mulder, "The Possibility Preacher," *Theology Today* 31 (July 1974): 159.
42. Schuller described himself as an "equilibristic thinker" in an interview with the author at Garden Grove, March 3, 1983.

Chapter VI
"The Theology of Self-Esteem"

1. Philip Nobile, "Rev. Robert Schuller: Possibility Preacher," *The Long Island Press*, Sun., Feb. 3, 1974, p. 38; and "Schuller Answers Critics," *Orange County Register*, Sun., March 5, 1978, p. A-3.
2. See Nobile, *op. cit.*, p. 38; and Beth Amante, "Saving His Flock from Garbage," *The Grand Rapids Press*, Sun., April 9, 1978, Wonderland section, p. 3. In an interview with the author (June 4, 1980, at Garden Grove) Schuller scored those critics who have portrayed him as a shallow thinker. "I think I'm deeper than all of them. I think they're shallow."
3. Schuller, "Door Interview: Robert Schuller," *The Wittenburg Door* 25 (June-July 1975): 11-12.
4. See Jan Roorda, "A Call to Live Joyously," *The Saturday Evening Post* 250 (April 1978): 120; and George Vecsey, "Preacher Who Pioneered Drive-In Religion Gains Followers With His Upbeat TV Show," *The New York Times*, Tues., Oct. 11, 1977, p. 25c.
5. Few religious books have had as wide a distribution; 250,000 complimentary copies of *Self-Esteem* were sent to churches and religious leaders, Catholic and Protestant, throughout America. W. Clement Stone, a consistent supporter of Schuller's ministry, picked up the tab for these hard-cover copies.
6. Schuller, *Self-Esteem: The New Reformation* (Waco, Tex.: Word Books, 1982), pp. 12-13.
7. *Ibid.*, pp. 12-13, 29-30.
8. *Ibid.*, pp. 25, 13.
9. *Ibid.*, p. 25.
10. *Ibid.*, pp. 174-75.
11. Quoted in Schuller, "The Theology of Self-Esteem," *The Saturday Evening Post* 252 (May/June 1980): 43. See also Schuller, *Self-Love: The Dynamic Force of Success* (Old Tappan, N.J.: Spire Books, 1969), pp. 15-24.
12. "The Theology of Self-Esteem," p. 43. See also *Self-Love*, pp. 15-24.
13. *Self-Esteem*, pp. 30-33.
14. "The Theology of Self-Esteem," p. 44.
15. *Ibid.*; and *Self-Esteem*, pp. 33-34.
16. "The Theology of Self-Esteem," pp. 44, 87-88.
17. See Schuller, panel discussion, "Self-Love: How Far? How Biblical? How Healthy?" *Eternity* 30 (Feb. 1979): 21.
18. *Self-Love*, pp. 25-27.
19. "The Theology of Self-Esteem," p. 88; and *Self-Esteem*, p. 15.

20. *Self-Esteem*, pp. 54, 53.

21. "The Theology of Self-Esteem," p. 88.

22. Schuller, *Peace of Mind through Possibility Thinking* (New York: Jove/HBJ Books, 1977), p. 34.

23. *Ibid.*; Schuller, panel discussion, *Eternity*, p. 23; Schuller, "Why Bob Schuller Smiles on Television," *Leadership* 2 (Winter 1981): 30; and *Self-Esteem*, pp. 65, 126-28. Here Schuller criticizes "historical theology" for failure "to make a distinction between 'Adam's sin' and 'Original sin' " (p. 65).

24. *Self-Esteem*, pp. 65-66; and *Peace of Mind*, p. 34.

25. *Self-Esteem*, p. 127.

26. Schuller, panel discussion, *Eternity*, p. 24.

27. *Self-Esteem*, pp. 67-68; see also "Why Bob Schuller Smiles on Television," pp. 28-29.

28. Schuller, "If Christ Were Alive Today . . .," in a collection of essays edited by Janis Johnson, *Ladies Home Journal* (Dec. 1977): 62; and Schuller, *You Can Become the Person You Want to Be* (Old Tappan, N.J.: Spire Books, 1973), p. 123.

29. *Peace of Mind*, p. 182; and Schuller, panel discussion, *Eternity*, p. 23.

30. "Why Bob Schuller Smiles on Television," p. 30. See also *Self-Esteem*, pp. 14-15, 127-28.

31. Schuller, "If Christ Were Alive Today . . .," pp. 62, 64; and "Why Bob Schuller Smiles on Television," p. 30. See also *Self-Esteem*, pp. 126-27.

32. Schuller, "If Christ Were Alive Today . . .," pp. 62, 64.

33. *Ibid.*, p. 64; see also *Self-Esteem*, pp. 159-61.

34. *Self-Esteem*, pp. 158, 74.

35. *Peace of Mind*, p. 34.

36. *Self-Love*, pp. 74-85.

37. *Peace of Mind*, p. 161.

38. *Self-Love*, p. 73.

39. *Self-Esteem*, p. 104.

40. *Peace of Mind*, pp. 161-62; see also *Self-Esteem*, pp. 102-103.

41. *Self-Love*, p. 84.

42. *Self-Esteem*, pp. 101-102; and *Peace of Mind*, p. 162.

43. Schuller, panel discussion, *Eternity*, pp. 21-22.

44. Schuller, *Move Ahead With Possibility Thinking* (Old Tappan, N.J.: Spire Books, 1967), p. 53.

45. Schuller, panel discussion, *Eternity*, pp. 21, 23; and *Self-Esteem*, p. 75.

45a. Schuller, in an interview with the author at Garden Grove, March 3, 1983; and *Self-Esteem*, pp. 39, 102.

46. *Self-Esteem*, pp. 107-109.

46a. *Ibid.*, pp. 109-113.

47. *Ibid.*, pp. 150-51; and "The Theology of Self-Esteem," pp. 88-89. I have chosen to elaborate five theological precepts which Schuller introduced in "The Theology of Self-Esteem" (1980): Theologies of Communication, Evangelism, Social Ethics, Economics, and Government. In the last chapter of *Self-Esteem: The New Reformation*, Schuller added the

Theology of Mission and eliminated the Theology of Government.
48. "The Theology of Self-Esteem," p. 88.
49. "Why Bob Schuller Smiles on Television," p. 30.
50. "The Theology of Self-Esteem," p. 88.
51. *Ibid.*
52. *Peace of Mind,* pp. 47-48.
53. "The Theology of Self-Esteem," p. 88.
54. *Ibid.*
55. *Self-Love,* p. 71.
56. "The Theology of Self-Esteem," p. 88. See also Schuller, "An Open Door to Prosperity," in *The Ten Best Messages* (Garden Grove: Hour of Power, 1980), pp. 54-55.
57. Schuller warned of the potential sins of capitalism in an interview with the author at Garden Grove, March 3, 1983. Schuller has invited a broad array of successful business persons to appear as special guests on the "Hour of Power." Many others have been cited in his books and sermons as prime examples of the scars to stars success motif. Schuller has established close ties with a number of America's most prominent capitalists, including Jay Van Andel and Richard DeVos of the Amway Corporation and the Chicago financier, W. Clement Stone.
58. "The Theology of Self-Esteem," p. 89.

Chapter VII
"The Gospel of Success in American Popular Religion"

1. Donald Meyer, *The Positive Thinkers: Religion as Pop Psychology From Mary Baker Eddy to Oral Roberts* (New York: Pantheon Books, 1980), p. xv.
2. See Richard Weiss, *The American Myth of Success: From Horatio Alger to Norman Vincent Peale* (New York: Basic Books, 1969), pp. 3-15.
3. For an analysis of Franklin's success ethic see Richard M. Huber, *The American Idea of Success* (New York: McGraw-Hill, 1971), pp. 15-22.
4. See Roy M. Anker, "Popular Religion and Theories of Self-Help," in *Handbook of American Popular Culture,* vol. II, ed. M. Thomas Inge (Westport, Conn.: Greenwood Press, 1980), p. 290.
5. Russell H. Conwell, *Acres of Diamonds* (New York: Harper and Brothers, 1915), pp. 18, 20-21. Huber supplies an important analysis of Conwell and his famous sermon, *op. cit.,* pp. 55-61.
6. Quoted in Huber, *op. cit.,* p. 124. See also Anker, *op. cit.,* pp. 291-93. For an introduction to New Thought see Horatio W. Dresser, *A History of New Thought* (New York: Thomas Y. Crowell, 1919); and Charles A. Braden, *Spirits in Rebellion: The Rise and Development of New Thought* (Dallas: Southern Methodist Univ. Press, 1963).
7. See Anker, *op. cit.,* pp. 292-93; and Sydney Ahlstrom, *A Religious History of the American People* (New Haven: Yale Univ. Press, 1972), pp. 1020-21.
8. See Meyer, *op. cit.,* pp. 33-40; and Anker, *op. cit.,* pp. 293-96.
9. Quoted in Charles S. Braden, *These Also Believe: A Study of*

Modern American Cults and Minority Religious Movements (New York: Macmillan, 1949), p. 136. See also Anker, *op. cit.*, p. 298.

10. Quoted in Charles S. Braden, ed., *Varieties of American Religion* (Chicago: Willett, Clark and Co., 1936), p. 150. See also Braden, *These Also Believe*, pp. 144-79; Ahlstrom, *op. cit.*, pp. 1027-29; and Anker, *op. cit.*, p. 300.

11. See Huber, *op. cit.*, p. 135.

12. Prentice Mulford, "The Necessity of Riches" and "The Religion of Dress" in *Your Forces and How to Use Them*, quoted in Huber, *op. cit.*, p. 137.

13. Ahlstrom, *op. cit.*, p. 1030.

14. Ralph Waldo Trine, *In Tune With the Infinite: Fullness of Peace, Power and Plenty* (London: Foulis Publishers, 1897, 1926), pp. 30, 207.

15. Anker, *op. cit.*, p. 299.

16. Ahlstrom, *op. cit.*, p. 1031.

17. Quoted in Ahlstrom, *op. cit.*, p. 1031.

18. *Ibid.*, p. 1032 note.

19. An illuminating chapter on Peale has been included in Huber's volume on success, *op. cit.*, pp. 314-40. The standard biography is Arthur Gordon, *Norman Vincent Peale: Minister to Millions* (Englewood Cliffs, N.J.: Prentice-Hall, 1958).

20. Huber details the astounding success of Peale's publishing ventures, *op. cit.*, pp. 316-17. See also Anker, *op. cit.*, pp. 301-302; and Lewis Schneider and Sanford M. Dornbusch, *Popular Religion: Inspirational Books in America* (Chicago: Chicago Univ. Press, 1958).

21. On the relationship between Peale and New Thought, see Anker, *op. cit.*, p. 301, and Huber, *op. cit.*, p. 324. Peale wrote in 1956: "I had long observed the practice of such religious groups as Christian Science, Unity and Metaphysical organizations. I observed that they all outlined in a simple one-two-three form, the 'how' of the spiritual life" (*Christian Herald* 79 [Feb. 1956]: 66). One of the chapters of *The Power of Positive Thinking* was titled "Inflow of New Thoughts can Remake You."

22. Peale, *The Power of Positive Thinking* (New York: Prentice-Hall, 1952), pp. viii, xi.

23. *Ibid.*, pp. 203-205.

24. *Ibid.*, pp. 36-41.

25. See Weiss, *op. cit.*, pp. 227-29.

26. But see Richard Quebedeaux, *By What Authority: The Rise of Personality Cults in American Christianity* (San Francisco: Harper and Row, 1982), pp. 88-94. Quebedeaux maintains that both Peale and Schuller are able to affirm "all the traditional Calvinistic doctrinal requirements of the Reformed Church in America" (p. 91). With reference to Schuller's thought Quebedeaux asserts that "the classical Christian symbolism remains intact; only the existential meaning of that symbolism is changed" (p. 91).

27. Quoted in Ronald Yates, "From Outdoor Theater to 'Cathedral'—a Religious Success Story," *The Chicago Tribune Magazine*, July 27, 1980, p. 23.

28. Schuller, "Self-Love: How Far? How Biblical? How Healthy?" panel discussion, *Eternity* 30 (Feb. 1979): 21.

28a. Schuller, in an interview with the author at Garden Grove, March 3, 1983.

29. Some of Oral Roberts' most familiar epigrams are revealing: "Something Good is Going to Happen to You," "Expect a Miracle," and "Our God is a Good God." A short but perceptive analysis of the recent ministry of Roberts is found in David Edwin Harrell, Jr., *All Things Possible: The Healing and Charismatic Revivals in Modern America* (Bloomington, Ind.: Indiana Univ. Press, 1975), pp. 150-58.

30. See Cynthia R. Schaible, "The Gospel of the Good Life," *Eternity* 32 (Feb. 1981): 21.

31. Nathan Hatch, "Purging the Poisoned Well Within," *Christianity Today* 23 (March 2, 1979): 15. In the concluding chapter of his recently revised edition of *The Positive Thinkers, op. cit.*, pp. 336-67, Donald Meyer suggests that evangelicalism is "The Old-Time Positive Religion." For an interesting assessment of the "success evangelists" from an impeccable evangelical source, see Schaible, *op. cit.*, pp. 21-27.

Chapter VIII
"Assessing Schuller's Message"

1. Dennis E. Shoemaker, "Schuller Shooting," *Theology Today* 31 (Jan. 1975): 350.

2. In Marshall Berges, "Arvella and Robert Schuller," *Los Angeles Times Home*, Dec. 12, 1976, p. 46.

3. Schuller, *The Peak to Peek Principle* (Garden City, N.Y.: Doubleday and Co., 1980), p. 61.

4. This subtitle served as the title of an article which Browne Barr wrote after attending a growth institute at Garden Grove. See Barr, "Finding the Good at Garden Grove," *The Christian Century* 94 (May 4, 1977): 424-27.

5. See Shoemaker, *op. cit.*, p. 354.

6. See "Door Interview: Robert Schuller," *The Wittenburg Door* 25 (June-July 1975): 14; and Schuller, *Your Church Has Real Possibilities* (Glendale, Calif.: Regal Books, 1974), pp. 112-28.

7. See *Cathedral Chronicle* 5 (Sept. 1981): 2. Financed by Hazel Wright of Chicago, the organ was manufactured by Ruffatti of Padua, Italy. The instrument has "223 ranks and a total of 13,000 pipes ranging in height from 3/8″ to 32 feet!" (p. 2).

8. Information about the ministries is obtained in a large fold-out publicity pamphlet produced at Garden Grove and entitled "Crystal Cathedral Ministries: We Must Survive and Thrive in 1981!"

9. Barr, *op. cit.*, p. 425.

10. It is difficult to prove that Schuller attracts a larger share of the unchurched than most television ministers, but this conclusion may safely be inferred from the fact that he draws a higher percentage of his audiences from less heavily churched areas of the country. See Jeffrey K. Hadden and Charles E. Swann, *Prime Time Preachers: The Rising Power of Televangelism* (Reading, Mass.: Addison-Wesley, 1981), p. 60.

11. See "Hour of Power Rated Number One," *Cathedral Chronicle* 5 (Sept. 1981): 1-2; and "Robert Schuller Wins Largest TV Audience," *The Church Herald* 40 (March 4, 1983): 22.

12. Barr, *op. cit.*, p. 427.

13. Schuller, *Self-Esteem: The New Reformation* (Waco, Tex.: Word Books, 1982), pp. 12-13.

14. Schuller, in an interview with the author at Garden Grove, March 3, 1983.

15. Schuller, *The Peak to Peek Principle*, p. 32.

16. See Phyllis Mather Rice, "Robert Schuller: Man With a Mission," *Your Church* 24 (Sept./Oct. 1978): 8.

17. Schuller, *The Peak to Peek Principle*, p. 29.

18. Schuller, *Self-Esteem*, pp. 117-21.

19. See Thomas Wolfe, "The Me Decade," *New York Magazine* (Aug. 23, 1976): 26-40; Peter Martin, "The New Narcissism," *Harpers* 251 (Oct. 1975): 45-50, 55-56; and Christopher Lasch, *The Culture of Narcissism: American Life in An Age of Diminishing Expectations* (New York: Warner Books, 1979), esp. pp. 17-103.

20. John R. W. Stott, "Must I Really Love Myself?" *Christianity Today* 22 (May 5, 1978): 34.

21. For a massive compendium of much of the recent research on self-esteem, see Ruth C. Wylie, *The Self-Concept: Revised Edition*, vol. 2 (Lincoln, Neb.: Univ. of Nebraska Press, 1979). Some of these studies are cited by W. Glenn Wilder, "The Search for Self-Esteem," *Journal of Psychology and Theology* 6 (Spring 1978): 183.

22. Nathaniel Branden, *The Psychology of Self-Esteem* (New York: Bantam Books, 1969), p. 110.

23. Anthony A. Hoekema, *The Christian Looks at Himself* (Grand Rapids: Wm. B. Eerdmans, 1975), p. 16. See also William M. Counts, "The Nature of Man and the Christian's Self-Esteem," *Journal of Psychology and Theology* 1 (Jan. 1973): 38-44.

24. Schuller, "Self-Love: How Far? How Biblical? How Healthy?" panel discussion, *Eternity* 30 (Feb. 1979): 23.

25. Hoekema, *op. cit.*, pp. 18, 23.

26. Schuller, *Self-Esteem*, p. 39.

27. Reinhold Niebuhr, "Impulse for Perfection and the Impulse for Community," in *The Godly and the Ungodly* (London: Faber and Faber, 1958), p. 120.

28. It is believed that these verses served as a hymn in the early church. See Henri Nouwen, "The Selfless Way to Christ," *Sojourners* 10 (June 1981): 14. (Nouwen's translation.)

29. Karl Barth, *Final Testimonies*, ed. Eberhard Busch, trans. Geoffrey W. Bromiley (Grand Rapids: Wm. B. Eerdmans, 1977), p. 37.

30. See Schuller, *Self-Esteem*, p. 65; also Schuller, "Why Bob Schuller Smiles on Television," *Leadership* 2 (Winter 1981): 29-30; and Schuller, *Peace of Mind Through Possibility Thinking* (New York: Jove/HBJ Books, 1977), pp. 33-34.

31. Schuller, in an interview with the author at Garden Grove, March 3, 1983. The phrase is from John R. Mulder, Schuller's professor of theology.

32. Augustine, *City of God,* XIV.13. Quoted in Reinhold Niebuhr, *The Nature and Destiny of Man,* vol. I (New York: Scribner's, 1941), pp. 186-87 note 1.

33. John Calvin, *Institutes of the Christian Religion,* II, 1, 2, ed. John T. McNeill, trans. Ford Lewis Battles (Philadelphia: Westminster Press, 1960), pp. 242-43.

34. For a discussion of the "self-serving bias" see David G. Myers, *The Inflated Self: Human Illusions and the Biblical Call to Hope* (New York: Seabury Press, 1980), pp. 43-120; and David G. Myers and Jack Ridl, "Can We All Be Better than Average?" *Psychology Today* 13 (Aug. 1979): 89, 95, 96, 98.

35. Schuller, in an interview with the author at Garden Grove, March 3, 1983.

36. Schuller, *Self-Esteem,* p. 104.

37. Calvin, *op. cit.,* II, 1, 2, p. 242.

38. Quoted in Nathan Hatch, "Purging the Poisoned Well Within," *Christianity Today* 23 (March 2, 1979): 15.

39. *Ibid.*

40. See Beth Amante, "Saving His Flock from Garbage," *The Grand Rapids Press,* April 9, 1978, Wonderland section, p. 3.

41. Schuller, in an interview with the author at Garden Grove, March 3, 1983.

42. Paul C. Vitz, *Psychology As Religion: The Cult of Self-Worship* (Grand Rapids: Wm. B. Eerdmans, 1977), p. 27.

43. Schuller, in an interview with the author at Garden Grove, March 3, 1983.

44. See "Door Interview: Robert Schuller," *op. cit.,* p. 11.

45. Vitz, *op. cit.,* pp. 33, 44-49, 91-105. The Rogers quote is taken from his *On Becoming a Real Person* (Boston: Houghton Mifflin, 1961), p. 122.

46. Hatch, *op. cit.,* p. 15.

47. See Richard Weiss, *The American Myth of Success: From Horatio Alger to Norman Vincent Peale* (New York: Basic Books, 1969), pp. 195-240.

47a. For a discussion of this research see David G. Myers, *Social Psychology* (New York: McGraw Hill, 1982), pp. 95-100.

48. For general studies dealing with the relationship between the mind and the body, see Norman Cousins, "The Mysterious Placebo: How the Mind Helps Medicine Work," *Saturday Review* 4 (Oct. 1, 1977): 8-12, 14, 16; Leslie L. Iversen, "The Chemistry of the Brain," *Scientific American* 241 (Sept. 1979): 134-49; Richard Restak, "Psychochemistry of the Brain," in *Mind and Super-Mind,* ed. Albert Rosenfeld (New York: Holt, Reinhart and Winston, 1977), p. 88; Solomon H. Snyder, "Opiate Receptors and Internal Opiates," *Scientific American* 236 (March 1977): 44-56; Mark R. Rosenzweig, Edward L. Bennett, and Martin C. Diamond, "Brain Changes in Response to Experience," in *The Nature and Nurture of Behavior,* ed. W. T. Greenbough (San Francisco: W. H. Freeman and Co., 1977), pp. 117-24; and Arthur C. Guyton, *Human Physiology and Mechanisms of Disease* (Philadelphia: W. B. Saunders, 1982); Herbert Benson, *The Mind/Body Effect* (New York: Simon and Schuster, 1979); Kenneth R. Pelletier, *Mind as Healer, Mind as Slayer* (San Francisco: Robert Briggs Associates, 1977); and

Norman L. Mitchell, "You Are What You Think," *Ministry* 55 (May 1982): 26, 27, 29. Many studies seem to demonstrate the relationship between chemical changes in the brain and physiological functions. It is difficult, however, to determine whether attitude changes affect chemical levels or whether changes in the brain's chemistry produce a change in attitude. Much more research under tightly controlled studies will be needed before that question will be satisfactorily answered.

49. Schuller, *Peace of Mind*, p. 108. Capitalization is Schuller's.

50. See Schuller, *You Can Become the Person You Want to Be* (Old Tappan, N.J.: Spire Books, 1973), pp. 39-40, 65, 122.

51. See Schuller, *Self-Esteem*.

52. Schuller, *Your Church Has Real Possibilities* (Glendale, Calif.: Regal Books, 1974), p. 128.

53. Schuller, in an interview with the author at Garden Grove, March 3, 1983.

54. Schuller, "I am the American Flag" (a published transcript of a message delivered from the pulpit of the Garden Grove Community Church, Garden Grove, Calif., 1972), p. 5.

55. See *Cathedral Chronicle* 5 (Sept. 1981): 1.

56. Schuller, *God's Way to the Good Life* (Grand Rapids: Wm. B. Eerdmans, 1963), p. 84

57. Schuller, *Self-Esteem*, p. 29.

58. See Acts 2 and 4, for instance.

59. See Shoemaker, *op. cit.*, p. 355.

60. Schuller, in an interview with the author at Garden Grove, March 3, 1983.